SELECTED POEMS

ERIC WALKER
SELECTED POEMS

Edited and with an Introduction
by Raymond Foye

Afterword by Neeli Cherkovski

Raymond Foye Books
New York

Published by

Raymond Foye Books
The Chelsea Hotel
222 West 23rd Street
New York, NY 10011

www.raymondfoye.info

To his mother, Diane Walker Murray

CONTENTS

INTRODUCTION: ERIC WALKER (1964 – 1994)

IT BEGAN as a kind of fairytale life in poetry; the young man from the provinces arrives in San Francisco to meet his mentors: the Beat poets of San Francisco and Berkeley. It was 1981, he was seventeen, he slept on floors, begged food, bummed cigarettes, and in the morning, left behind scribbled poems that delighted and amazed his hosts. These early years were filled with promise, joy, and exuberance, but there followed in his twenties a chaotic descent into mental illness. The poetry and madness, in classic fashion, often went hand in hand. A dozen years and five hundred poems later, he was found hanging in a prison cell, aged twenty-nine.[1]

I knew Eric mainly by reputation, having moved away from San Francisco by the time he arrived. Stories about him were swapped around by other poets from the very moment he appeared. I came to know his work from the five marvelous chapbooks published in his lifetime by Tisa Walden's Deep Forest press.[2] I met him on occasional visits, and like most I was struck by his ethereal beauty, physical frailty, emotional intensity, and of course the poems that flowed from him so naturally, sometimes two or three a day. At any given moment he would retreat to a corner of the room where he would gather the ideas and images swirling around his head, and he would commit poem to paper in about the same amount of time it takes us to read them. Each poem is a kind of emission, an unbroken flow from start to finish.

Then he would disappear for a month or two, returning to his mother's home near Santa Cruz, or his father's cabin in Richardson Grove, on California's central coast. During

---

1   For an extensive account of Walker's illness and death, see Richard Rawles' excellent "The Fall of Euphorion: The Wrongful Death of Eric Walker," Spectacle, vol 1, no 2, Spring, 1988, p 37-58. Reprinted on www.bigbridge.org. Rawles, a social worker and mental health professional, was also a personal friend of Walker's from the age of fourteen until his death at twenty-nine. Walker was incarcerated because he violated a restraining order. Many of his friends doubted whether his death was in fact a suicide. The truth will never be known. His family was given a wrongful death settlement.

2   The books are: *Night's Garden* (1983), *Helen* (1986), *Jonah's Song* (1988), *Through the Day* (1990), *Notes on a Surrealist* (1993). The Deep Forest archives are housed at the Bancroft Library at the University of California, Berkeley.

this time he would type up his poems and assemble them into individual volumes of two or three hundred pages each.[3] These visits back home also gave him a chance to wander in his beloved redwoods, where he found his inspiration and solace: "I learned poetry from watching nature," he once wrote. Ecological imbalance is one of the chief concerns in his poetry, and in the final year or two of his life it became his main concern, as he witnessed the horrific destruction of old growth redwood forests in California.

His school years were desultory and filled with boredom, aside from his extensive readings. An exception was a first prize in a local poetry competition, which he won with a poem titled "Sweet Carrion." Walker's most enduring influence was Rimbaud; at fourteen he encountered a biography of the poet, *The Day on Fire* by James Ramsey Ullman, and he immediately understood his calling. At times he considered himself the reincarnation of Rimbaud, and the "disordering" of the senses became an imperative.

Eric's first mentor in life was California's great poet of the primal forces of nature, the Dominican, Brother Antoninus (William Everson). Eric sought him out at the University of California at Santa Cruz, auditing his classes while still in high school. He quickly earned Everson's esteem, immortalized in an enthusiastic comment scrawled on a class paper that he had a promising future as a poet—an artifact Eric saved his entire life. Eric never enrolled at UCSD; his grades in high school were poor and so were his economic resources. But he told a friend that if you pretended to be a student everyone just assumed you were, and for a time he even lived in a college dormitory.

A pilgrimage to San Francisco and Berkeley was inevitable, and within a short time after his arrival in 1981 he met all the poets of North Beach and Telegraph Avenue and joined their society. It was a remarkable time for poetry, with many of the principal figures of the San Francisco Renaissance

3 Some of these volumes are titled: *Schizophrenia, Hearts and Freeways, The Rational Response, Subterranean Heart, Hell's Children, The Heart's Assembly, Thoughts on Dying.* They are preserved in the order he left them, at the Bancroft Library.

14

still active and accessible, and a vital younger generation followed and honored them, in their own very different and unique ways. It was the classic *La Vie Bohème*, with the cafes crowded by day and the bars by night. There were regular open mics and communal dinners. Little magazines included *Beatitude* and a monthly newspaper, *Poetry Flash*. Small presses included Tisa Walden's *Deep Forest*, Kaye McDonough's *Greenlight Press*, and of course Lawrence Ferlinghetti's *City Lights Books*. Eric dove straight in.

He was taken seriously from the start. Amongst his elder poets he was held in particular esteem by Bob Kaufman, Philip Lamantia, and Howard Hart. Younger poets who mentored and took him in were Neeli Cherkovski, Paul Landry, Rosemary Manno, Jack Mueller, Julia Vinograd, Tisa Walden, Kristen Wetterhahn, Rudy Jon Tanner and many others. Eric was lucky to have a large support system, since even a day or two with him was enough to leave one frazzled. He was a regular at the weekly readings at the Spaghetti Factory on Grant Avenue, and he made the rounds of half a dozen other open mics over the course of the week. He also read his poems on the street for food or money. Over the years he was banned from many of these venues for unruly behavior, in one case setting his poetry manuscript on fire as he was reading it.

He seems to have absorbed nearly the entire arc of post–war poetry in the Bay Area. The Sufi wisdom of Daniel Moore's two City Lights books (*Burnt Heart* and *Dawn Visions*) are an important influence, as is the surrealist vision of Philip Lamantia. He absorbed Kirby Doyle's rugged poems of the California continent before the arrival of man, and likewise Howard Hart's elegant lyricism drawn from the French poets Reverdy and Éluard. Even Richard Brautigan, living in North Beach but largely inaccessible, makes an appearance: "just so Brautigan in his trout-fishing jacket/ had a vision of American weeds, transfigured/ the sleight of hand of a magician in hiding."

Walker's tribute to Bob Kaufman ("The Ancient Rain") reprinted in this volume is a fine snapshot of this period. It is also one of the only first-hand accounts of this remarkable African-American jazz poet. Walker is, in my view, the main protégé and successor to Bob Kaufman, and that in itself is important. Walker's deep devotion to the elder poet is evident, as is his insight into the many forces that brought about this wrecked but still defiant individual—forces which one day would also prove Eric's own undoing: poverty, police, jail, mental hospitals, and the mutilating forces of corporate capitalism upon the weak and vulnerable. The struggle for freedom and social justice is vital to Walker's poetry, and it is rooted deep within his psyche. The poem—no matter how whimsical—was always an act of personal and mental transformation intended to bring about the same in the reader. And like Kaufman's, nearly all of Eric's poems are in fact quite accurate descriptions of real events, subtly veiled behind obliquely surreal imagery.

Walker's many madhouse poems address the breakdown of human worth and social value with a clarity that to my mind is only equaled by the poetry of John Wieners from the early 1970s, when the Boston poet became an activist for the rights of mental patients, following numerous incarcerations. Walker knew the work of John Wieners well, and his poem "The Asylum of Dull and Dark Sad-Eyed Angels" is his own version of Wieners' powerful poem "Children of the Working Class." The condition of insanity (his own and the world's) is a constant theme in Walker's verse. Of the asylum poems in this collection, most were composed during more or less rational periods of recuperation. However there are quite a number of sprawling texts not included in this volume that offer a view from the other side of the mirror: prose poems and manifestos written during periods of derangement, where the schiz-analysis of society and its ills are presented with frightening power and poignancy.

Cruel and dangerous confrontations with the law (shoplifting food, vagrancy) and the mental health establishment (incarcerations, debilitating medications) inspired many remarkably cogent manifestos from this period where he explores the dynamics of debt, war, media propaganda, and government control—particularly as it bears upon the powerless and vulnerable, the artists and dreamers. In these works Walker repeatedly evokes the figure of Artaud, whose work he was acquainted with from Jack Hirschman's City Lights anthology. Hopefully these challenging texts and manifestos will be published in the coming years.

Another influence Walker absorbed was the popular music of the 1960s and 70s, which contained much fine writing that brought poetry back to its Troubadour roots: Joni Mitchell, Jim Morrison, Syd Barrett, Crosby, Stills, Nash and Young—are all cited in his work. But by far his most important influence in this regard is Bob Dylan, whose gentle lyricism, vivid imagery, and ardent emotion is everywhere evident. Those familiar with Dylan's work will find subtle references throughout this book, particularly to the albums *Desire* and *Street Legal,* with their imagery of Tarot and the occult, or the Gospel albums, forged in a fiery Christian mysticism first awakened in Eric by his teacher Brother Antoninus. There were years when Eric consciously adopted Dylan's style and dress, and in times of crisis Dylan becomes the touchstone, evidenced by several poems in this book written in the form of fan letters (the epistle, or poem-as-letter, is one of his favorite forms). I think it is fair to say that Rimbaud, Kaufman, and Dylan, were his holy trinity.

There is always a cogent political worldview in Walker's poetry, even at his most irrational. Like Allen Ginsberg's epic "The Fall of America," or Bob Kaufman's "The Ancient Rain," Walker's poetry describes the last gasps of the American empire, choking on militarism, media brainwashing, and petrochemical pollution: "The light is wisdom, night is falling on America, / could it be we are losing our wisdom?" In his poem "The Tao in America," it is expressed as a need for a yin-yang balance between Industry and Nature, Capital and Emotions. "Poem for Jesse" (i.e., Jesse Jackson) presages the election of a black president. And in "American Roads," circa 1993, he eerily predicts our present moment: "...on the carpeted floors/of Jerry Lewis's giant telethon, corporate stars fight/ for the presidency,

17

weird Trump pulls out a flush-straight/ against the hijinx of passionate parties..."[4] The brutality of power is his final subject.

His final years were spent in institutions and halfway houses. Often for months at a time his only visitor was his mother. On March 13, 1994, Eric was found hanging in his cell at the Humboldt County Jail, aged 29. He was the third inmate to die there under suspicious circumstances, and eventually a wrongful death verdict was issued to his family. His work fell into obscurity for the next two decades, remembered only by those who knew him, many of whom are now themselves passed on.

Eric Walker's entire surviving output is a little over five hundred poems, and several hundred pages of prose, all now preserved at the Bancroft Library at the University of California at Berkeley. Not every poem is successful, but every poem is stamped with his own unique sensibility and style. One must at times make allowances for the youthful imitations and experiments, or some of the excessively sentimental poems written in the throes of love. In the end, he is a poet of poetry itself.

Some of these poems were published during Eric's lifetime by the poet Tisa Walden, in *Beatitudes* and *Deep Forest*. The rest were preserved by Eric's mother, Diane Walker Murray, who stored them safely for two decades, before they came into my hands through a truly strange set of circumstances. I was living for several months in Kathmandu in 2014, and on the very evening I completed editing Harry Smith's lectures on Native American cosmography, there was an auspicious full moon (Hanuman Jayatri) coinciding with a lunar eclipse. That night I dreamt of Eric: I was walking around the stupa in Bodnath with hundreds of other devotees. Suddenly, in my dream, I spied Eric up ahead wearing monk's robes. I was shocked to see him after so many years. I caught up with him and confronted him. "I'm fine now," he said. "Everything is alright with me." Then

---

4   The poems "The Tao of America" and "American Roads" are not included in this volume due to their length. They can be consulted at the Bancroft Library, or via communications with the publisher.

I lost him in the crowd. It was a strange dream because in the previous twenty years I had hardly thought of him at all. When I returned to the U.S. a few weeks later, a psychic named Laura Lynne Jackson told me that a friend of mine—a young poet who died in despair twenty years earlier—had been reborn an incarnate lama in Nepal and was now living a happy life, having repaid a cosmic debt. The following day I received a call from Eric's mother, whom I did not know (she had been given my name by Tisa Walden). She told me she had been diagnosed with a terminal illness and would I accept a shipment of all of his manuscripts and notebooks? Over the next two years Eric's brother, Scott Walker, diligently typed all of the work, and provided valuable editorial insights, and research. Thus, in this strange way, this book came to be.

Raymond Foye
Woodstock, NY 2018

ALL I HAVE IS POETRY

Nothing but the summer bent
on destruction, honesty demeaned
by cruelty; a cold joke abducting love
in its tremulous arms. And I have
held her before in such quietude,
with a longing that could reach
out and touch the sea in an incriminating
silence. Life is gone, after touching
its dusky fingers on the glass,
sealess and broken. No one will
know me from the edge of
this dark, all is gone, faraway,
like a crowded room of mirrors suddenly
vacated. Death soars like an Osprey,
hovering in my direction, I am hurt,
but recovering. Dreams fade into
brilliant flower-stems, pressed
in forgotten manuscripts. And
when I finally die the world
will deny me due process, because
all I had was Poetry to wrap
my corpse in.

AMERICAN HEART

Strange bed to sleep in
eyes of pain & marked cards
      endless halls hummed
like old hymns of broken words
mumbling into the night
      I ran from city to city
in old shoes of endless summer
laughter followed in my head
those were the depressing years
      I slept upon the great summit
willed my road in heat & like a dog did beg
on streets of rain & cried coldly:
"I am a ghost & no carpenter's son!"
unholy wine tasted my lips
and the cities burned with wet tears
& she there the sister that never was
left me in autumn's drunken light
an american queen that I adored
turned like an endless quest
to find only her skin of ashes and blood
      fell then to her death & troubled like a child
that could sing no more
      an avenue ghosts & cantankerous old me
in my haven crumbling
that I had read the words written on walls so
bituminous with cackling leaves of crystal teeth
the words read simply: Have a nice day!

AMERICAN MEMORIAL

"When men bathed in perfume and practiced the hoax of free
        speech"

Bob Dylan

                    Rivers, steel flow
of eyes & Emerson techniques of silver stallions
bodies immersed in clay, sunken pirate ships
and loving the Spanish tongue of drunk spoons
                            bending loose as tigers
            feelings of the beloved riots
of Watt's Tower and demon bridge
suffocating on the silent mass of tongues
slang surfacing from Walden Pond
                    The dead streets of Ancient Rain
brought upon by black Bob in boots of silent leather
coming from behind the velvet hat of a
            ranting King Fisher
After Olson we dive for the bloody lion
                    caped in glassy water
when time spoke of human attributes that the blind could
not see that strange machine
                                dancing barefoot in Haight & Ashbury
with a dog barking on a leash & the scream of Joplin's purse
                                    filled & drugged leather
pills, suffocating in simmering mechanics of Love & Body
politics where Malcolm burns his draft card
& dreams come lucid thanks to Martin's bullet proof new
Church of the Hendrix experience raving Purple Haze
he walked his days under African skies
                    a private Angel raised from
the black & silent pit of prisons uniform in
blue phantom blue at rooftops aimed against the destruction
of america and raising the dead street in sullen escapades
            of personal glory &
he walked against the trial of tears and half jew beat black
angel of visions where the Golden Sardine stretched its
magic eyes
                            & Howl's birth a tempered

On The Road visitations of the black crime of Antonius
a Brother to the Dominican conscription of the fallen house
of cards where Peace calls its dirty names at the grateful
                              Wares of War and its giant machinery
fastened to a tongue of J.F.K. missionaries looking for
a blind fuck of Marilyn who died for the sins of many
and fast addiction turns to the sound of birds worn on
heavy shoulders of the white & blissful creation
of Madonna's heavy make-up, the post-fun of a blue painting
of the Spaniard and whose brilliant corpse raised in Solitudes
Crowded with Loneliness, this is a memory of Him
        who praised
the upside down culture of Beatitudes and plastic pigeons
filled with beat-up drug-stores I stayed with him telling
him of the virtues of Jazz-born sweat, eyes black marbles
and the old man dead, now there is nothing but Mr. King-
fisher
                    & the Old Man of the
Sea stretched in canvas to sell American blues
and the Old Tiger burns bright in the night sweating
crimson fingers in the second coming of King and his marches
through suburban L.A. fortresses
                              where does the Lion & Lamb lie down
with mercy clouds of broken shops & fire & tongues too still
for Rodney's bones to mend on the engine of self-hatred
the fast free-way slam of speed, junk, crank & rock
hard nose-bleeds where does the lamb burn its white wood
and women bleed from their other face
                              abortion & quietude of forces
where trembling his hand engenders the Flood
with faceless light, only the mirror of angry war-ships
on crisis from the Dominican Republic blue flag
and God sins against the animation of War
            we hurting in silent rain
                    from which LINCOLN Commandeered
his share of burnt daisies
& fastened his upper lip
                                        w/ dew-drops
to recognize the black flame burning inside
the old poet's throat.

                                        5/31/93

THE ANCIENT RAIN
"Creation is Perfect"

Bob Kaufman

I first met Bob Kaufman in North Beach at a poetry gathering. The old Spaghetti Factory was a place poets had gathered for over forty years; it was Beat, with old wicker chairs hanging from ceiling and painter's memoranda decorating the walls. They had an open reading every Thursday. It also was a bar where you could hang out and drink when some poet was on in the back stage that you didn't care for. It was a restaurant that prided itself in Italian cuisine, and had the best garlic bread that I've ever tasted. The place was buzzing on Thursdays, and usually more than forty poets had already signed up when you got there. Bob was a black jew, who had acclaimed fame back in the late 50's and early sixties. He had walked a tight-rope of racism all his life, and when I found him he was living in an all black ghetto. He had emphysema and also brain damage from getting beat up by the cops, and getting strung out on booze, thorazine and amphetamines. I remember the night he packed the backroom with poets waiting to here the legendary Bob Kaufman read. He recited the Kingfisher poem and from memory, and chanted it like a man coughing to death. His health was so bad, and he looked like a someone who had been to hell and back. The legend of Bob surrounded him like a nimbus. On thing I realized in listening to him recite, was that he was a real poet beaten down by society; the potential fate of us all. He had two things that made him almost a martyr he was black and jewish, with an obvious talent for changing words into whips; white tipped and staining bodies of a thirst for scarlet. He had lived life on street drugs and booze and he had barley survived life's catastrophe. I still remember how he chanted, with snot running down his face, looking like a sculpture of pain; as though some one had divided the good and the bad times, and left him naked, swimming in bone, cold and tragic, yet at the same time familiarly warm. His face was truly black, not pale brown, and he wore an artist's cap, and looked very poetic with his black beard trimmed with gray. He was as I learned latter a proud and dignified man beaten down by society till there was nothing left in the end but a bed that he

25

could die in, and a woman who latter would discover his smiling corpse. He was like a phoenix with his words rising out of the pyre of his own soul, and reaching people with meaning and depth.

To be a man of words is to leave this world with a gift, that is the sum of your worth. Bob left me with more than a gift, he left me with silence he had fought for so long. I lived with Bob, and experienced his broken soul, that once, so long ago he had poured out of humanity. I remember during the nineteen-eighty-four elections, the man laying in his hammock of peace, making it known to all that his sickness was not a disguise. The depth of Bob was his sinking frog eyes, that had once leapt above the world like a paratrooper: Like unleavened bread Bob had seen that too much consumption little by little burned into his palms and shaped him into a poet of darkness, one that cries out in the night against the criminality of chemicals and materialism. He searched deep into the jazz tones of his spirit and found there a wrecked ship smelling of brandy and cigarettes. Bob was a naturally loving man, and he always knew when he was being used, he stuck to himself, watching T.V. on his death-bed. The silence Bob had partaken of was merely the realization that something higher penetrating his injured skull like a voice faraway, or a stillness that comes on sudden like sudden death.

The Ancient Rain was the title of Bob's last book. It in my opinion it is the most important work. It is a vision of emancipation, like the old Pharaohs, and even like Noah with the vision of Holy Justice coming down from heaven. For a man who had one too many nights of black hatred, one too many unforgiveable beatings, he shows us that there is a kind of justice coming from on high, and that creation is truly perfect. The poet is the receiver, it is him that talks and bargains with God. Though death has triumph, the poet defeats it with a mirror of words that hypnotizes the clouds. Like a moth attached to the fire, Bob lived his life seeking truth. The truth he eventually found was cable T.V. I remember one night I was upstairs talking on the telephone, when I hear Bob's rough voice calling to me. I came down to see what he

26

wanted; Barney Miller was on, our favorite program, and he wanted us to watch it together. It became a ritual; late night T.V. Though Bob could barely hear, he kept his concentration on the screen. I also found out that Bob liked Bob Dylan. The stereo was always tuned to KJAZZ, Bob's favorite music, he had lived jazz and fought for jazz to liberate his soul. The Ancient Rain would come softly in the night and bless his skeleton with tears of holy wonder. It is worth saying that Bob loved people, especially children. I remember one day I found him at the gate waiting for me to come home. I handed him a stuffed rattle, like a two handled gavel that a jester would carry: I found it on the sidewalk that afternoon, and Bob accepted it. When he came back into the house he had a big smile and his eyes were sparkling. I asked him what he had done with the stuffed rattle, he said: still grinning "I gave it to the baby next door." There was indeed a baby and a single chicano mother who I had talked with a few brief times. Bob loved this baby, as Bob loved the words that broke his silence. At the final hour comes the final wisdom; Bob was prepared for his death. One night when I was asleep on the couch, Bob had gotten up and started a fire in the kitchen... "The lights, I wanted to go out and see, but I couldn't find the flash light..." Bob explained himself. Can we imagine what the lights he was talking about in his mystic babble. Perhaps they were real, just inflated in Bob's imagination, or like the Ancient Rain, a symbol for the search for purity in words and thoughts, the Lights were present that night. To open up to the possibly of prophecy is to begin to read poetry for the first time, getting goose-bumps up and down your arms, to be filled with the power of myth, which still in this modern age provides us with sacred food that fulfills us with our spiritual hunger running savage, and our knowingness small and humble. Everyone knows that poets aren't perfect, either was Bob; but according to Bob, Creation is perfect. It is a funny fact that a man who had fought so much in his life would in return give peaceful odes to silence. The cold facts were Bob's addiction to drugs and booze. Everyone knew that Bob was a man of the bars, and under booze he wrote his most lucid poems.

Bob's son Parker did not maintain a close relationship with his father. I never met him, but I did know his mother. There was a separate reality between the two men, as both dealt with racism in their unique way. Bob dealt with it by putting on the face of the tragic clown, his son had no talent I this way, he was a dancer and expressed his creative energy through his body. Bob was an intellectual, and kept himself locked up in his own head. Though once, a long time ago, Bob had danced on the tables of the Bagel Factory, reciting poetry for the cops. There had been rebellion, as though he too had defied his father, and chose to go out to sea at an early age. The poet hands us a cross of flesh, mixing pleasure and pain, waiting and wondering what the Ancient rain might do when it comes back to earth. The first and the last, the omega and the Alpha; Black-Man had been first once, first created, and now God would seek out his original people from the darkest part of the city. Even pride had been broken, and self-pity had opened up, asking would you wear my Eyes? Yes Bob we will never wear your eyes, one day after the Ancient Rain has subsided: "A fish with frog eyes, Creation is Perfect."

ASYLUM

Faces of broken ash; dreaming
on the edge of burning breath;
steel rain falling; falling, falling,
heavy sided, clear-cut, engulfing...
When you're lost; when your shield
is down; when you can't face the
pain surrounding you; when nothing
is easy; when the ink leaves scars;
when nobody wants you, and you're
wearing away like sand crushed by
the sea; fingers crawling; dizzy
headed and weary of the sundial of
your breath; empty handed and hungry;
trying to make sense out of a
senseless struggle; slowly movement
stirring and fomenting; tragedy,
insanity; debris, draining and spent; a terrible
Summer where the uneasy sea
uncovered the shore; bloody red pilings
slipping beneath a tidal moon; eclipsing
hangover melting in pure drunk sound;
feeling paranoid, watching for the guilt-
ridden flock to up and fly away;
sleep in a fox-hole; a fountain parting
its narrow folds to slip and drink from
itself; pouting and staring at the
dark midnight; a fist a shouting; a
brainless sea of self-fulfilling
prophecy; a fever tilted at
the edge of mad Asylum; Asylum of
mediocrity and senseless suffering;
Asylum of stinging fingers and needles;
of punches never thrown; of cigarettes
bummed from nobody; of smoking
saliva and heavy coughing; of
camouflaged phlegm with blood
and a bingo of hands all marching
on tiny rain-drops of sickness; of

love that is distempered; of absolute
poverty and the fingers of the rich;
while we in pot-holes give ourselves
the finger, while draining the puss from
our minds; slamming doors; doors slam
in faces narrowed by hallways; pinched
by angry shadows; feelings bypass
each other; technicians of the
insane, hike through hallways; walk heavy breath down
corridors pretending they are important, top-chested
clowns glued to their key-chains; while
loud music profanes their uneasy silence;
laughter drawn from lunacy; while the Intercom
plays God and MC of the circus; hiding tattooed
razors in silent pockets of the disabled veterans;
averted eyes advert gazes and stoned and
indifferent hallways shifty like eyes flashing in the dark;
feelings pressed against heavy sighs; pill
box rattles, containing our scrambled
brains; hatred bleeds hatred; fights
scorpions at night; imaginary or real
green phantoms explode beneath the bed;
leaves blood on the window-sill; tries to
calm itself in restraints... Train, col' train
of summits unbranched; cold head track
of dawn pill-eyed and staring at the
medicine counter; swearing a
constant hello at empty strangers barking
words at walkways and invisible operators...
Asylum, O sad col'train coming slow up
the mountain, blowing its mouth like
an uptite rain that nobody
can stand; empty of wine or reason,
yes a cold rain stands between us
and the secret airs of that magic elixir
that's never been found...
Caffeine highs in secret bathrooms
filled with instant coffee, sighs and
struggles to keep its breath before
the ambulance comes; degradation

and over-simplification of the problems
society won't deal with; lock the spiders
in their room and see them weave their
webs, struggle and cut themselves on the
thread; Hotel California plays on the
radio as we pretend to check out
on suburban vacations of bad acid
and bad beer; and still those voices
are calling from faraway; bad bloody
nightmares imprison us with our own devices;
dreaming of running, simply running,
nowhere to nowhere like a connect the
dot picture; the fervent blood runs
deep calling collect on nervous mirrors;
the telephone rings but nobody answers
it; a party called a party; but
nobody could get through; dancing
on the ceiling; our days outnumber
each other; a dapple gray on the slickness
of linoleum; a cold tit complaining of
Pete Wilson's outlaw band of restitutional
scavengers; obsidian clowns beg for coffee
in restaurants that poison your mind;
divas hold conference in pajamas out in the
pouring rain; while Doris does a back-flip
 through the front-desk; this is the
House of the Rising Sun filled with tranquilized
animals sedated by the turbulent Generals of Dawn...
Drugged mirrors vacated like empty palaces
stand in wait for us; while Humpty Dumpty
accidentally cracked his skull while leaning backwards
on a brand new white plastic chair...
Hidden motifs meant for nobody, but modified for the
Times; like a
crazy popcorn glue that nobody can
sell; manifestoes of grief written
on toilet-paper and given to
the insane to blow their noses on...
Obscene gestures in hallways condemned
with traffic; ugliness bares its brooding face;

sitting pretty on a precipice of Reason; soon
the parody becomes too much; exiled nerves
trying to take a piss and listening to voices
at the same time; a triumph of days and hours
marked red on the calendar; exterior; interior
rain, more rain in the naked boudoirs of the
already excavated saints; Christ has a passion,
and it bleeds sin; horse-play and disease in the
unrecorded memories of unlisted rainbows; rediscovered
in mental-health of crimes of colored pills all numbered
and well charted; menstrual blood overflowing in a
sea of senseless paper; pushed by brooms bristled
with dysentery and as a logical as a tuberculosis;
sleeping anarchy breaks windows when it wakes up angry;
fist wave in silent reprisal; while residents
scream with dark pleurisy in their lungs...

Doctor Placenta doesn't give
shock-treatments no more; he is placidly
senile, with his white-trimmed beard and balding head;
I'm sure he has ulcers; he just sits there whispering:
"Uh Huh!" at all his patients, while sky-diving
behind his glasses. His penned voice quakes
a little as he writes in the chart;
yes sir he is an astute one; always
prepared to medicate his verbs when
they are out of order, or trapped in
his own saliva; he eats out and
works odd hours, like Sundays and seven-to-nine
on weekdays; charts orange colored lay stacked behind
the desk; these charts contain the secret of our
illness and we're not even allowed to read them;
charts everywhere; like naked children
playing with big plastic balloons; while
Doctor Placenta urinates in the staff toilet
while dreaming profusely of a red Volkswagen
double parked at the curb horn honking...
Voices roaring; cantankerous as ever; me in Group 1;
the Conference Room door closed; singing in the groin;
sly laughter biting at my nails; hold it in; do not pay

the consequences of a friend's death; after all it's not
my fault; doing loss like some strange ballerina
dancing over a counterfeit grave-yard; orange soda
in hand; I imagine his mexico hearse in the mountains
with cancer; demanding the song to rise from a raucous throat;
midnight and sinking like a beggar into his easy chair; writing
the poems that haunted everyone; aware of the pain; a ceaseless
dance hunting the sorrowful throat of whispers so strong that
everybody could hear them if they owned ears to listen;
sipping at tequila with dead fingers smiling at the
pen clicking beneath him; owned too by Asylum's charm...
Now Death takes him to his villa; now he is in
true Exile from Life... a nervous Hiroshima of the heart
lingers in me like the aftermath of a nauseous
hangover; O' Lord hide me; wanna dance cool baptism
slow and angry; a tiger caught by its tail is
convincing enough; robbed of its courage it goes nowhere;
but inwards it claws at its own entrails; O' Asylum you
have robbed the sky of its beauty; and it is raining;
Lord it's raining cats & dogs; it seems like it will
never stop... The usual butterflies came as I pushed the
buzzer to be let back in; a stomach full of them; out drinking
coffee on an hour pass; I return and its ad nauseum
all over again; the actual poison ingested is better
than the fever's edge; ever congested tubes full of
orange-colored liquid; poison drains from our toes and
 finger-tips; dark murky saline solution teaching our
thoughts to wash away like the rain; a still echo
of Don Juan running through ghettoes of
obsidian night; shaved ice, a tattooed hand rises to
replace the other; psychic skyscrapers in monument of Man's
triumph over death; though the clocks move in wreckage
teaching us that pain is everywhere; Paul's death; a vanishing
Sun; popcorn in the rain; outlined like a Volcano of past
experiences...
Death & a carton of cigarettes & two dollars & sixty three
cents... Makeshift ears prowl the night, listening to voices
and lurking in shadows... Dark beards
of pajama dawn lurking like a Foster-freeze add...
jerking off in the vanishing beds; dogs run free; but

the children of insanity cannot stop the blood from
running through misty veins; cages and lock
ups; and technicians of the insane highway
held like small suicides in mirrors of eyeless
windows, with hell to pay, for the museum of gods
is truly the weird tragic guilt of the americana;
at fault; no one; fumbling the ball at third quarter;
it's a game of costumes; a new hide-a-way of truants
on the run; the owned and unwed mothers of destitution
habituate the babies of chemical dependency; some say
a genetic disorder; though always it is the free song
of open hearts that dance through the institution; one
by one, open to Asylum's arms.

BEATING A PATH TO YOUR DOOR

I am a lover of other things,
I came to place my orphan
in your hands,
to tell of midnight
an how I love it
with these hands motionless,
placed over back-bone
touching your skin with
a razor-edge disappearance,
feeling your warmth melt
into me,
you say we have an understanding,
I say these walls are cushioned
with leavetakings leave-takings,
like to break into your mouth
to say a word or two,
exclaiming "nice girl"
with an icy grin,
I melt the body of your taste
damned by its rainbow blood,
a queer coming with your arms
crossed and my fingers quivering
to know that crossing touch
that plays on the mermaid's body,
strangling in a street of noise,
loving nothing sacred.

BLUES

Feeling low down and mean,
wanna die wanna sing,
want those blues to dance
through the dam of my heart,
a trumpet of musical defiance
shapes the word of the Law,
definition: the blues are tonal;
an exponent of the bi-valves of
heart-shaped valentines in cool
black velvet, cold rhapsody
of blind heroin, tasted like
a drink of whiskey, melting inside
a carcinogenic balloon,
hands shaped like baseballs
pounding on the back of my head,
boot-calls come dancing, come crawling
across the living-room floor,
cement crying in footsteps of fever,
born naked in this bald fanfare
of rare exquisite flowers unfolding
in a vase signed by Picasso,
their sleeping tones creep steadily
into my woman's heart, step lightly
on warm-lipped brass blowing freely
upon the White Dream of concentration,
free at last to sing the blues!!!

BREAKING THE WALL

Changing the tides of history
they meet at the wall to dance and celebrate,
they look through the cracks
at a life once separated to its country, nation,
world. They make-believe like children
that there is freedom; freedom like a sledgehammer
falls and breaks chunks of concrete.
They are waiting for a better view,
to see one's neighbor, to call each other
mutual partners in the forming of governments.
United they look to a better future.
Much like us they reflect joy of knowing
a new freedom.
Somebody's hands are busy removing white
chunks of concrete. Goodby Goodbye separator.
Say hello to passports and freedom to wander.
Today we must also break the wall.
The wall between us and our children, lover or
landlord. The wall that keeps us trapped in a life
of labyrinths and shallow people.
We must break those white walls that surface
between us and friends.
Joyfully they break the wall.
Brotherhood is not "big brother" but that fraternal
understanding that shares a moment together in a
world of events.
This might be another event, but today it
Happened, the hole between east and west is much
bigger. We can see our way now. After all there
is just people, governments are illusions. People
choose where and what they must do.
Seek out your potential.
White brick falls. Celebrations ensue.
Bring hammers, chisels, bring your own two hands.
Together we must break the wall.

BROKEN WINDOW

The image infected
nude asylum of a
shattered place;
just the pull of a trigger
to warm the body,
feeling echoes misplaced
mirror driven into bone,
the lady in blue is dividing
herself again,
the holy mask torn
from the air,
the street filled with garbage,
chanting the bells toll:

morning is a broken record!

a fist full of glass
knuckle tender,
dealing with its belly-full,
seeing outward
the roar inside ourselves
stretches like an abrupt yawn
burrowing into the dirty windows
of the streets.

BUBBLE

Sometimes knife-edged
a slicing eye of glass
turned round in your warm hand
a cold phlegm separating me
like the curved glass
of a light-house tower
springing from your belly;
the crystalline bell
jumping
in your throat,
a phoenix splattered
wall to wall
in this open nerve,
to make the jump back
into the warm liquid
fountain in your forehead,
to say I have come
without coming,
to say the eye is really
the I, artifice of landscape,
broken butterfly machine
that cannot pump softness
of its wings
without first a few stiff
calculations, frozen bellies
of snow open up
in California tan hands,
a whole web of stamens
shooting yellow through
the brown of your face,
the target being no target
but the backside of a lip
with its flesh-pink honey-comb
worn smooth of this
skeletal forehead,
bitten sheath of darkness
in that I carry you,
a quivering calm congesting

an icy rainbow
that the hand bends from
to the spoon of this table,
open yellow root of my brain
ticking inside the beast of Light.

THE CAPITAL PUNISHMENT

They will kill me tomorrow,
or maybe next week,
they will distribute my bones
into various canneries,
but nobody will sing at my death,
they will burn my work with relish,
they will stamp on my blood, and
turn my words into slapstick,
the fat lady will dance with the Kaiser,
the broken skeleton will turn toward justice
but find only the misprint of his words
in the newspapers that cheat the dead,
wear a shroud white as snow,
I will live belonging to their assassins,
they slip below the water line,
they are the ones that must not understand
that God is the presence of life,
they cheat and lie and take profit
of a man's soul, and I am but meat
to be cleaned and sold and bid on
blind snow carved into the cold ruin
of a hopeless dream,
to stand like a four-legged tree
inside the dome of salvation.

CATCHING BREATH

After the first mouth
discovers the second mouth;
the way mammals do,
touching like water,
my mouth upon your mouth,
cupped around your secret flesh,
becoming,
the exchange of breath
like a sigh incomparable
to the wind;
what air are we taking,
each others,
the surreptitious grin
of another chin to chin,
we take, we give
to each other,
part of the current
is drowning in us,
is making itself known,
the flesh of your mouth
begins by knowing the flesh of mine,
the turn of air inside your lungs
like a fish breathing under water,
you give and I take this breath
held inside us,
stirring at the bottom
is a wind made from the darkest invisibility,
that these lips should hold on,
looking for the breath they cannot catch.

CHANGING SKINS

Walking with a stick of brass
calling up the dead
from a hot drum
played by the Sun
I am a sinking ship
a toy in the ether
my flesh is the burning sand
on a beach that has no shore
I am as the beach is, infinite
I have no place to go
a new moon has come
I sit behind its pinched shadow
with a necklace of shells
these are historic artifacts
time is a place far away
the human heart spills its blood
for a crowd of working ants
red bites on the fingertips
it is lonely with your soul
it never rains only clears
the clouds off the glass lid
of the coffin
the planes are coming again
they roar like mosquitoes
I am an oracle in need of food
on a love-seat that is barred
by the wind
it has a quilt and blanket
of fresh bone
I stand alone
War is a peaceful friend
A fight to the end
a loving wife, a life
turned inside out
a hand and a shout
I will never live, only to give
the first tap on the door
sequins stretched out

on the floor like shiny pennies
I am kicking the door in
Soon I will find out what's inside
the sea, the ocean
cartoons filled with sand
the jellyfish that has no bone
a star crushed in stone
we walk alive huddled like flies
around a dead seal
a fish that trembles is almost dead
a whale cast to the bottom of the Earth
is worn like an overcoat
given to Poseidon for his sail
he will go to the center of nickel
Walk the shallow regions
and roar with his mouth filled with foam
he is dressed like Jonah
for his long journey home
he dives beneath the flat sea
killing you and me.

CHECK-MATE

Sorry that you arrived w/ murder
in your eyes, leery of God and His
Omega wants, black Alpha, handsome
devil straight from two touch-stones,
one a tree made of sawdust, two
a jail made of night, the clay
never really left your fingers,
there darkness spent its warmth,
your frightened window, Equus became
a knight of smoke, slip sliding,
weary of God the devil, left
his guns on the mountain, long ago
they turned to roses, the machine
hid itself in a garden overripe
with fear, dancing its way to
destruction.

CHRISTMAS MORNING 92

Bringing it all back home,
Christmas in the asylum,
settled in the air is cold
and sheltered, there is a
component of silence mixed w/ joy
and grief, and anguish,
we are waiting to open our presents,
stacks of green and red boxes await us,
past eleven and the fury driven bows are
slashed and eighty-five mental patients are
busy opening their packages, listening to Deja Vu
on my Walkman, they're dragging their paper with them,
and it's simply crazy to watch them tear and rip
their packages, happiness comes in all colors,
Father of Woodstock you are here with us,
blind colors tasted from your eyes, butterflies
and star-dust, making new rules for the old year,
bellies and laughter and Santa Claus is a woman this year,
I know her, she is a group counselor, I have tasted good
cheer from the bottled rainbow, I have erased my mind
in a tasteless tomorrow, where is the wheel and where
is the blood? Shouting my name in the sky's clay,
dancing with memory on a sunstained lake, crying
inside a mirror of windows, surmising the
absolute terror of being alone, they are smiling now,
misplaced names in a bag of silk, and no one cares what
is happening in my mind, cat-calls and poisoned rivers,
they have burned and hurried my sanity in flesh and dreams
of diverse institutions,
with but one open call: Merry Christmas to All!!!
and for those who've lost their faith,
God is born again today, and we have all
been here before!

CIRCLES

In the dream I am watching a circle
turn inside out. I am at the window
and the streets are moving around
and around, there is a car slipping
underwater, the driver is very nervous,
we are going to a movie, there is still
time, though I am in Chicago and dreaming
of a World inverted like a lop-sided donut,
there is a man turning into a woman reading
Wilhelm Reich's Murder of Christ, he says
"It's a game which I love to play, and this
book has so much history..."
I stop him and look into his eyes, he is
a she and I double over, I was hit by a grenade,
my mind turned again like the circular Sun,
I am walking avenues of eastern Illinois,
I am playing a guitar while the girls begin
to undress, their breast are circles within
circles, and I touch the empty place between them,
I am standing on top of a giant store-front looking
down on the people, somebody says Jump! so I take
off flying, there over the crowd is another circle
spinning into infinity, and I am told to remember the
dream, that I cannot stop to enter the blue air
which is actually a circle within a circle, I stop
beneath it, wondering who is producing in this circular
orbit, and then I remember I am dreaming, somebody wakes
me up, I try escaping,
breath harder, heart-beats
inside the movement of the circle,
as I tremble with confrontation,
I am awake dreaming about a dream,
staring deep into the blond wind,
waiting to be taken away from here,
sad conclusion, the air stops me
from disappearing, I stand by the sea
watching the boats come in,
I am one of the drowning boats, my boots

made of soft leather, somebody is eating
an egg, I stumble across pages of sand,
am reawakened and told to turn over,
the doctor gives me a shot, it gyres
up my spine, and the circles begin
again.

CITY WATER

Serenity is Light transformed into liquid.
The eyes of the bridge are watching us.
A turbulent blue sitting in an orange Sun,
cascading through the shimmering gold of flames
tossed through waves of green immersed in the
tired turnover of cars passing us;
aqua colors curl their feet into socks of
crystal light, turbans of feeling etch in
the black water, smoke dreams in turning passages
of glassy silence; an otter moves distantly around
the swaying boats, masts lit by darkening shadows,
gloved in quiet reflective modes,
city water moves like a freeway without sound,
only the jetting hues pushed forward
in the timeless jaunt of pausing lights.

CLOSING THE DOOR

And I had a warm room
to sit quietly in, strangling in
a noose of books,
and a musical cat to sit and watch
for hours dance to sad-eyed lady
of the lowlands, and in the morning
when the fog came in, overlaying the redwoods,
I would sit deathly still,
hearing the silence engulf me.

CROSS-ROADS

These strange signs,
as though the laughter of lunatics
made the cold ground tremble,
here I stand in the asylum
with a week before my release,
I bargain, I am filled with inner calm;
to go to the peaceable kingdom where flesh
is the winding of a clock, or to spend the
nights in a steel cage, lost in the electricity
of ghosts, and I have a few questions to ask God,
why did you take away from me the fever of my blood,
and inside my broken soul I think that you have
given no mercy, in you who I trusted???
Mercy for you my poor girl, my sister of light,
waiting on the other side for me.
I peered into the dark cross-roads, one was meant
for me, and as I tread beneath the bushes that stain
your jacket with red and black berries, I avoid the
thorns of solitude, this manifest destiny of the
tortured and damned watching as I step on the delicate
flower, its ageless, and like a drowning man I hear
the drone of the sea, and the whistle of hot air popping
in blankets of sheltered seeds...
I have left you now, alone, with the court of justice
on neither of our sides, just spent watching as I travel
this road, this path I cling to, like water to mud.
And I see you vanishing in the darkness, budding fine

and stolid with the ghost of your memory cleaned and
learning from the path of footsteps in an endless darkness,
I take care of you and remember the promise we made to
each other.

DANCING ATOMS

Heroes of dust
you shall return to the earth,
the sky is dancing above your graves,
the ocean is spinning in your skulls,
look and love for one second,
one split second you live on this green planet,
the mirror of solitude reflects the action
of your wanting body,
now that dust and energy are but one
solitary hand, like the Breath of God
they answer your dissolute questions,
open your eyes and see the Tao
wintering in America.

DIVING UNDER

Precipice of skin mixed with clouds
teeth closed tight
world fixed beneath me
imagination's quest to find
what doesn't exist, the perceptual world
a cold blue hidden behind foam
aqua flowers rub raw against the chest
knees knocking cold
this is as physical as dolphins' speech
the clock is silver and hangs on the wall
the orifice opens and closes like
a giant eyelid filled with prismatic light
golden ball in which I push to make a narrow
passage of mirrored bone
going inward I hear the Giant's speech
like pillows of liquid genuflecting
physical birth is the round puff of its eyes
the closing of a great orgasm
purification round and still, shaking
in silent shock the walls bend
a bubble born under heat and shadow
mounts on a crest of clear sky.

DREAM OF A FRIEND WHO DIED

In it you appeared sexy,
you bared your breasts like cauliflower
with the quick turning smile of a crab leg,
you disrobed and tossed your head sideways,
I was going somewhere, you stopped me in the door,
made me want to feel your breast smooth as glass,
gulp with my fingers like open wounds,
you sat crossed legged and smiled
about indulgence, you moved your white hands
into a cold dark place, your brother, of course
you had no real brother, but the younger sister,
well anyways he cried for you and picked up the
blankets off the floor, I tried breaking into that room
your warm smile turned into cooked meat,
your body went to snow, then ice,
I climbed the shallow waters
hoping I might touch the knee of winter
without freezing to death,
I was living on the streets again, I was borrowing the
floor of your room, I slept while you played with
your rat, letting him climb all over your hands,
I smoked plenty of cigarettes and stared deeply
into the ocean of your throat clapped still and
inward belly, that latter meant to secure a kind of
photography to keep what was left,
though conscious of the loss, I still dream
that you stepped back into my life,
loving you.

FIRE

Dazzle, sharp burning
acrid smell of flesh on the grill
twinkle of light in the dark air
burning sensation of night's warm hair
blind touch of flame's hand
a ghost wavers in the candle's light
blue smoke slowly rises to the ceiling
a cart dark as night suddenly burst in flames
powerful lightning burns a snag oak
fire magic chanting its intelligent beauty
a flick of shadow in the gray evening
turns purple then red then orange
covering the whole sky with painted colors
these rituals of looking into the hearth
to see the aged god rise and take birth again
bright as day it turns out of the ashes
that burn with black death
it jumps, it flies with powerful breath
turns the air bright red and moves its monstrous
head upward into heaven
tied to the dark he wavers
while the eagle eats away
at his stolen breast
burned to an unimaginable crest
of arcing flam without knowledge
of why or how he came.

FORGOTTEN BIRTH

Funny I don't feel it,
the suffering is only a lonely star
upon the dried earth,
she is a quarter moon
filled with the fragrance of perfume,
funny I can't see it,
not that fantastic sea filled with
blind fish, not this fatalistic Sun
shinning again on the new horizon,
funny I don't know you,
not on this sacred ground,
an acoustic guitar is playing through
the tide,
I remember only the summit
with its untarnished wind,
with its white clouds;
not in memory the season dwindles,
but before the pain of summer's jets
pressing in on the skin's soft paws;
earth, air, fire,
funny I thought you were coming back,
but nobody said you'd stay behind,
nobody told me about you,
well it's about time you remembered,
that day language sweltered,
that day of the beast and the lamb,
somebody called it Babylon,
funny I don't recall you being there,
no not in the catacomb of silence,
funny I don't remember you standing in the cataclysm,
if only for a day or maybe an hour,
I stopped seeing you,
all meshed in like a hammer of brilliance,
silence ended there,
and I am afraid to go further.

FORGOTTEN CITY

We live in a place
that is forgotten
like the old base-ball glove
you keep in your attic
this place is all but memories
City of no name
from place to place we go
carrying our mementos with us
selling our home for pocket change
living with the fact that we are
helpless as kittens
at least we appear that way
in the welfare line
each evening we are brave and scared
of the night
that falls in hushed shadows
no blankets on our bed
just a sleeping bag and the silk of the rain
washing our heads clean
we are the homeless earthquake
that the nation can't quite deal with
with our broken eyes and supper of salvaged stew
we walk the vacant streets filled with rubble
we are the outcasts that the newspapers refuse to publish
though our plight is common we are known simply as
    the "no-names"
of Society and the forgotten ones who live on hunger
    and solitude
the derelicts who raid dumpsters and the cold cigarette
smoking hospitalized that has no one but cancer to call
a close relative
wizards of the night we play with sparklers and cook up meat
to feed our dogs
in the light of broken moon we see them
the place of forgotten enchantment of lost solitude and
    pitiless time
the forgotten city and its inhabitants
carried together like baskets of baked bread

this bread we break is for the people we have forgotten
all those misplaced lives that exist on the Edge
living in a single place multiplied by horizons
beneath a forgotten shore.

GAMES

Birth hot flesh like paper-dolls
in the wind, a flash of dreams
supplicated by the first blue star,
meandering in the winter cold,
breaking sticks and dreaming faceless
eyes like ponies bold in peony
precious love set you down,
this is the whole pie
of innocent apples,
freeze-tag in the tall meadow,
frozen footsteps turn yellow
in the morning Sun,
a closet full of lions
and a mirror cast in childhood wonder,
a broom of white smoke, and candy
set in green ashtrays,
this is a children's summit,
so say hello to the giving of winter,
bright blue eyes smile at me,
and I am happy teasing those
blonde curls,
a parade of stuffed animals
and a taste of backgammon
the firm hold of cribbage,
twenty and one ways to play solitaire,
bright and happy puzzles of love,
the range of good-times and the mellow Sun.

GAMES II

The games people play,
I am dancing hereafter,
playing hide-n-seek without myself,
what a fanfare of tools,
wreaking havoc in the night we the
fantasy of what it is to be human,
you ask me of existentialism,
everything stands on its own,
everything has stood that way for years,
the Universe is alone with itself, aloof
and wayward it crosses boundaries,
we are its boundaries,
it is communicating through us everything,
she the communion of Spirit & Body,
woman of the compliance of dreams,
she the union of flesh, of eyes and ears,
mouth and nose...
                              searching for a locus
I spend my energies on surfaces,
a game of Chess, today I check the soup
of your eyes, salad and croutons,
enchilada supper,
food hangover,
pot-smoke
resounds in the horizon,
I kiss you for the first time and you say "Locento"

sorry I have never done this before
water-heron circles with beak laden with fish,
eyes of seals pop up distantly in the water,
life resounds in this moment,
stillness, all around us is music,
the music of the spheres,
language cries inside out
a pop up
mirror that
disintegrates with the overflowing beard
of water,

instigate
rape
a blind thing, a tasseled darkness
overflowing like some flag of masculinity,
your friend with Blake and Angeldom
sweet asylum,
hungry for words.

GIFTS

Teaching the hands
to bend,
the dog has a headache,
the laughing man stretches
forth his umbilical cord
of fine silver,
the shine of it forever,
a cold shape in the distance
shaken off the tree
of light,
from Nazareth we go forth,
from the rock
our hands shelter
from the hurt stone
whose sides bleed a river,
a whale cast in the
iron rust of your fingers,
the chrysalis has sprung a nest
in the bones, from Sinai we come
the gifts of the river
are stones to build a house,
a boat with a broken engine
a straw horse, a fish found
in the tossed silver wave
placement of hands.

GREEN EYES

Lying still
the long years
waiting and sounding
a hollow back of clay
little house with
the green-eyed girl in it
tight buds surviving the frost
cling to the rain.

A tired lap bruised and broken
like the sea flashing its body
knit together with pebbles
and shells round as water
and petal free
the hard coast of facts
where a whale stumbles
in terrestrial darkness.

Sonar of blue wind
the long arms meeting
in undercurrents
the measure of roots
the wind and the heart
like the clasp of two hands
a fragile base
located in stone
a river wild as foam
a shape of it alone
coming up for air
outside the great sea.
Linger and retreat
to the song of leaves
fallen and crushed on the ground
how can I explain you?
the sad child of sleep
wakes and calls your name
like hooks cast in water
drowning divided sunlight

the quietude of space inside
the shell is a clear echo
of your body
the glare and sting of light
sinks down further
below the anchored shore
I wake up tumbling
turning my eyes like a sharp axe
to the rocky sand.

Girl and lady of the vine
umbilical and fine
let me make a chain
of rust and star-fish
my age like a bracelet
of salted wood drifting
near the rod that marks
the ocean preserved
like jelly in tight bubbles
through the floor which can see
behind itself a stranger
of skins reflected
a bell sparked with fire-light
round as the shape
of your knees.

It is everlasting
this house and carriage
the ghost-bent bone
of the primal waters
the smell sparked into life
the kind hollow hand
is a cup of sweetness
held out to the icy halls
of the dead.

A stone is a voyage
a dropped marble catching the eyes
of children and men
a woman hunts for the first

silent reflection
the good earth becomes
a tunnel of light
to see where it fell
the stone darkens to rust
set in tears.

This is the voyage
a golden fleece
laid in the ground
a surrender to the first
thing named
seagull shaking the water
around her
the broken face comes
in circles
the narrow eyes
whisper back.

GREEN

When we think of colors, when we breathe magic
we consume nature, we conjecture,
we look for the talisman that will make us well.
This is the same with the 'green' politic.
Throughout this country there is a forest,
a green root,
not ideals that trap us in blind paradox,
but a grass movement spreading like wild fire
throughout the land.
Our Mother is green, green is the earth,
green is growing through the dirt.
Green song of the early Spring, the stem
and the carpel are green, green petals
of the wildest flower of all
mother's apples ripe and green pippins,
used in a pie that is all American
surfacing from land itself,
people wearing green t-shirts, gathering signatures
on a green ballot.
The World is coming to its senses,
it no longer sees in red.
There are vines growing over the cement silos.
A blackberry bush grows right next to the nuclear power plant.
Across from PG&E's defunct plant there are horses and
    sheep grazing
one the green land
America is green.
Vote green.
The verdant forest is watching us.
We have trespassed against the wilderness.
With our weapons we see only the nightmare of this world.
Dark sojourn into a dark world where memory has collapsed
Remember our green Mother, the Earth loves green.
Sky blue and green the grass.
We can no longer follow Hitler.
The Earth spins in its green orbit.

HAPPY BIRTHDAY

Tonight is my 29th Birthday,
I have celebrated, seconds, moments,
years, treasures, belongings, creations;
I have melted in windows of tears,
dark pilings, I have made magic
a real thing, and dealt with the awesome
Archetypes of the Tidal Unconscious,
I have not forced Beauty though,
but wooed her with a passion,
sought her in everything I did,
I did not curse the darkness but lit
a match to it to see it up close,
I stand at the Turning-point, whistling
my love songs for you, oh sweet and comforting
woman, let me taste your lips again,
embrace and smell the warmth of your body;
fierce passion breeds in me,
I stand at the Cross-roads, distant,
starving for love, she the special fantasy
explodes in my mind, she the sentient one,
is the depth of a river wild and full of torrents,
just a moment ago, tongue on tongue, mouth sweet
belonging to just us, could it be you?
Questions, endless questions,
I see you in the morning of my birth,
kind mother who brought me life,
and father, you in your fishing-cap just taking
off for Carlotta, thank you for the seed;
I am the seed! I carry it in me,
I exist everyday for the smallness of change,
coffee in the birth-mart, existing
like a pirate alone with his flag or marx-manship,
I exist the ploy of a terrace of blond beauty,
a pageant of casual remarks,
and you lady who kisses like water,
I shall dream of you tonight, I will lay down
my arms and rest in the birth-song, taken
to the path that I only cannot pertain,

I am the key, the seed of all belonging,
Happy Birthday.

09/08/1964

HELEN

So you went & slipped into the mirror,
you really did it, you finalized the project;
my spirit is a piano, you see me running
in place of your tawn dirty feet,
why did you jump it so heavy and hard
my egg shell honey, the sweet cream
of my nightmare, the tasteless joke
of your dead-weight fixed in the air
in the smell of a jettisoned flower,
your face hit humming up
a whole hive of bees;
your damn mental body stuck in my mind,
and your loving still twisted into my fingers,
and the savagery of your eyes
(brown and soft marble)
echoing the dim mirror of my wandering
life-hotel lips praising your existence
in the foggy redwood air.

HORIZONS

The sky is blue
like shattered crystal,
through old growth
I can see the purple smile of clover,
its body green with the underside lifted up,
the red cedar climbs its way through thickets
of sharp-eyed nettles,
the sea is a body of love washing up on the rocks,
this is the North-Coast, nobody has seen this kind
of beauty, except when hiking in nature,
the western hemlock has its head bent down,
its trunk is large and knotty,
the spider-web has its silken threads around a huckleberry
the light moves in it, new horizons for the slender legs
of God's favorite tapestry,
nature is eternal, it leads to the sea,
the ocean wanes and waxes like the moon,
with tides that take it from high to low,
everything is a delicate balance,
white foam awash on the beach,
otters and whales swim to the touch of hidden currents,
these are horizons yet to be explored,
the peace of nature is not remembered when man
takes his machines and drives them into the forest,
horizon of the new day, bless us now
before we sleep and forget,
man is very forgetful, mankind must remember
his birth-right, and the natural upbringing of
his soul, horizon unfold
now and forever.

HOUSE OF ANCIENT RAIN

Dishes done, old man sleeping in
next room, his black eyes mumbling;
music of shadows and running water,
white walls speak twisted nerves,
ice clicks in glass,
these walls so nakedly white
have a ghost walking in them,
of splattered color, and I reminded
of the ancient rain in this sunny afternoon.

IF

The World will blossom if
we turn around, if the light
doesn't scare, if nothing is
sacred except tomorrow,
if the evening falls softly,
if the daylight is mirrored,
if the only open scar is
a bottle of seltzer,
if the stars go blind,
if the warm caress produces
a living hand,
if people shout to be free,
if the leftovers can be salvaged
by a blue justice system,
if the music does open to
the quick and helpless light,
if we begin again to taste
with tongues of pleasure,
if the protests scare enough people,
if memory is the seed from which a
blossom grows.

ILLUMINED BODY

I sing the body electrified by night
and the quiet turn of smoke and eyes
of flesh burning inside the tears of
tortured love, burning inside out
and the paper bird lives inside the
Illumined Body, a boy wrote of illuminations
from which the sighs of lepers relinquished control,
slept inside the mirror's tantalizing privacy,
turned a new edge on those Paris streets,
shocking the body into crystal illumination,
strange metamorphosis climbing the wind,
turgid like a prayer of golden smoke,
burning little with its snow white countenance,
swollen eyes dug deep into the clean works of white
and black, dove upon which the sea whispers its name
in the straw darkness, that which beneath the whittled
wheel of Time is this strange light coming from behind
the veil where he wrote his stranger's songs illumined
in a body of pure light, sung softly to the sleeper's
ears.

THE IMAGE

Born in the Womb with life's limbs,
drawn from the light by basket-weavers and cave-painters,
this fleeting thing caught in a permanent stasis,
kept in a circular forest with brightness as Lord,
the scene of woman giving birth to an icon of trust and fear,
the warm blood like chalk and canvass,
the emptiness of the Universe filled with pictures of
a smaller universe, like pulsars trembling in a sea
of color, the film is ready for the projector, the Image
stands by itself.

Looking at the thread of Life on explores the smallness
of something so huge that it cannot be fathomed,
like the birth smile of pain in a woman's cheeks contracted
like the pleasure of sex, but small eyes quivering with
ancient life, and that is the smile of the dying, those
infected with death and the last gasp of the organs, the
dying breath of life, that is the smile of a Madonna or a
Buddha, who sees the Image of a star, the life's organs
pulsing through the veil, penetrating Time with its pensive stare.
A smile of weeping, a torture of understanding, a thing filled
with birth and death, like the winsome lips of a skeleton,
contemplative and frightening.
The Image is born laughing, crying, sighing and spitting,
it is raised from the grave knowing, testing, and turning
from the emptiness to Life, its fingers shake, its eyes
pop out, it is eternal and one with Life.
There in the darkness, in the seed spun from green apples,
there is growing the Image, transplanted in the skull of
an animal, born with eyes and breath, it is instilled in us,
and as the dying woman smiles, hope is born.
Framed in the nighttime, we see the stars in their webs
of light, and this follows us to our grave...
To touch, to belong to the world, the Image supersedes the
World,
Flowers and is born to the skin, while surviving Death.

IN THE MEANTIME

We reckon that evil will not last,
that good must triumph,
but in this wreck less World a
dark sleep comes to relieve the
standing guard, a hurricane of size
the torment, runs blue through silver
nails and trapped dreams;
a sky of turbulent blue
weakens the flesh, and seeking
the missile of heat in your body
flat like a board; lying next to
the house of cremation, spending time
with the undertaker's skeletons, you
sweet in the wine of dirt, you spell
your name like a lesson in tracing
the thin calm of your birth; a slip
of hidden smiles, where I caressed your
thighs with an open hand, and here in the
meantime we pretend that there is no flame,
only the smouldering ashes of a significant
offering, blue blood and the leftovers of
a kiss, watching the streaking night
undress in its hidden hotel-room
where we talk and strip like horses
in the mid-run, with sweating shoulders
and eyes of hidden mirrors, striking
sunlight against the broad-side
of a faceless tomorrow.

IN WAY OF AN INTRODUCTION:
LIVING WITH INSECTS

The Saint without a Halo loves all animals, including insects.
Their bright crisp bodies cry out in the intelligence of nature,
they are sophisticated, and are capable of complicated tasks.
They do not kill each other but rather work together to create
a better life for themselves. They fly, they buzz, they crawl,
they are naked sentient beings, their bodies are armored with
the earth, their treasure is the earth. Look at the miraculous
transformation of a butterfly, the smallness of a ladybug,
the skeletal remains of a potato bug, the moon-stained wings
of a moth; this earth is teeming with insects. There is a fear
of the primal beings that crawl on the earth, there the sting
of a yellow jacket is a warming of their power. The other day
I killed an ant, and while watching I saw this ant come up to
the tree where I killed it and try to take its body away.
It climbed around the dead ant at least eight times before trying
to pick up the body of the dead ant. He carried it maybe
   three inches,
gave up and went around the tree. He came back and
   began again
to carry the body of the dead ant, with no success he went away
and met with another ant. The other ant then came, picked up
the body of the dead ant and proceeded to carry it quite
   a distance,
across the grass, then across the sidewalk to the other side, some
three or four yards till it disappeared. What is incredible about
this story then the communication between the two ants. This is
poetry, the exploration of a new or a very old language.

     This poetry is the search of Life. If we are to live on
this planet we are to share it with the others. Insects I believe
are probably the most apt to survive on this war-torn planet.
The great Howl of destiny is with us, it is comic, it is
a red machine marching through history, like a pin-wheel
contained with the names of the dead and murdered children.
How can we stop this destruction, what does it take to say
never again, and who is responsible for the damaged earth,
the ravishing of our Mother??? These insects will survive

the holocaust, they will cast great shadows on the evening of their ascent. Time will tell who is the most intelligent and compassionate creature. They have civilization; not a crumbling society that has been vacated since the West began, but a true meaningful hierarchy, there are workers, home builders, and egg hatchers. They live below ground, surrounded by a catacomb of mysterious and very alive chambers. This civilization has been around for a very long time, since the beginning of the earth. Their smallness makes them very inclined to a destiny with the earth as the fruits of their labor. They are born in eggs, and they multiply constantly. For this we are afraid of their takeover, though it's bound to come. Insects work hard! They work at birth, and change into beautiful subjects of nature, such as the butterfly, or a bumblebee. They procreate in the chambers of the earth, and sometimes from the smallest come the largest; with their ordered social importance, they begin at a very early age serving their race. They see not like us, and they walk with many legs. The tiny pill bug is one of the most well built insects, it can curl up into a ball and protects itself from predators. There is communication unique to their species, such as the ants that I described, or the bees, with their honey-flower talk. It is the language of Nature, with its mosaic of vast truth covered in earth, or caught hugging the bright sky with tiny beating wings.

The Voice of modern poetry has been a freeing of the senses, and a preparation for the acceptance of Life on the Planet. Life is sending signals to us, and these bright enigmas cannot yet be interpreted by science. We are aware of the existence of the smallest entities, of the molecular build of the Universe, but we have not quite recognized this as intelligence. In fact there is no logical perception that has yet been brought into a perspective that these small sized creatures are truly intelligent, and what's more have compassion for each other and live an ordered and quality life. They die too soon, or they are pests, this is how we value the greatest species on earth. Insects are phenomenally ambitious in their take-over of the world, but because they see order in all things, they are waiting for us to recognize them. They see us, the so called 'giants', but they do not fear us, they know they are superior, and their innateness gives them the power over us that we cannot see, or refuse to recognize. They are building their civilization beside ours, and some day soon we will crumble and they will take us over. They are durable, fast at breeding, and genuinely curious. Someday soon a poet will learn their language and begin speaking it. Till that day the Saint without a Halo will struggle with divinity, to find the roots of this intrinsic intellect that moves all things. Till then the value of life must remain silent

August 1st 1991

LETTER FROM THE ASYLUM #2

Butter-scotch pudding and a make-believe dinner setting.
People waiting in lines to eat and drink. Over-crowded
hall-ways, and broken eyes staring into the gutter. Cigarettes
again and again, having no fun with the Vatican. Why and
how, and what forbidden sin? The full flesh of a face made
love to in the victorious mission of isolation. It is a
free-land, but where's the temple in here, where's the freedom
to worship God, without being wrung through the wringer.
The fierceness of my baptism leads me to believe that no
other person could shake that from me. Configuration of
stars in the endless void. Meal-times are like a free-style
cafeteria with dull and bland food. Sometimes, like Sundays,
we have meat. The roast beef tasted good tonight, the tortured
vegetables sang out, crying: "Don't touch me" and the peach
short-cake demanded a whole glass of milk.

LETTER TO BOB DYLAN

Dear Bob-
Throughout the years I have listened to your songs;
eyes spelling hymns that heard the inner Christ within,
songs like old friends; a poet by nature, I have been
interested in your development as a christian; I see
the World more and more like you; a spiritual catastrophe
that is also a war of mental and physical verbs, a sad
and disturbed rhythm of steel and flesh; a vast wasteland
of human values... I grew up in Santa Cruz, and split to
SF and Berkeley as young man driven insane by words...
Now I am living in a mental hospital in Eureka California,
and the days pass in the gloom of mental breakdown, the sad
reality that we are exposed to the blind and selfish truth,
that human-beings can be wreck-less, that they can be treated
like animals, and pushed through the system while sedated
on medication that makes them shake and talk funny...
I think of a young man who visited a sick old man and made
him happy; I am thinking of Woody Guthrie, who was probably
a greater influence on you than you even let on in your writings;
there was such a man in my life too... Bob Kaufman, beat poet
and black angel of Be-bop and Ancient Rain, was for me a profound
lesson in Truth... I first met him in North Beach when I was
eighteen, and later lived with him off and on for over three
years. Bob showed me that life meant as much as poetry, and
less than morals. Every action has a reaction, and he was
chemically addicted to cigarettes, alcohol and speed. He
spent his whole time smoking cigarettes and disappearing to
the bars. He was very sick, and I knew he wouldn't make it
much more than he already had. His silence was disturbing,
yet it was the very thing that fascinated me. How could a
man stay silent so long, without words, but maybe thoughts
and voices that lingered in his mental state, but not in his
spiritual vision of Life. I was extremely influenced by
Arthur Rimbaud's work, but Kaufman was even more intense;
a living exposure of the great fire that burns inside its
Prophets, distilling them and even driving them over the edge.
So my season was distinctly different, it had a meter and
a rhythm; like cats making love, it squalled, squealed, and

its stealth stole from me Life's magic. I learned that a man
is only what he believes in, it's the system that beats us
so far down, that we let go of even hope. To pacify the World
with songs that resist the furious flames with every lingering
rhyme, and subsist on candy-bars and celery sticks, that howl
like broken angels, in the subliminal knowledge of Life insisting
on its own brighter force, the slipping constantly over the edge,
where beauty is defined as anything and everything we cannot
touch, is truly the baptism of poetic excellence. Love is definitely
a four-letter word, and Christianity has adopted to its own
fervent distress and fear of a World that we are actually free
to believe in what we want to, and not what somebody tells
us to. There is no magic, other than this. And what of the
Ancient Rain? Burning and trembling inside us, is a collective
Will that is the most fascinating mixture of animal survival
and intellectual prowess. I should say: that to live one must
excavate the World of all its primary and basic passions;
then the absolute is not so scary; while trapped inside
us, distant and advanced to the point of belonging.
Where is the person who can say simply stating that
we are all the same, and yet different... Estranged as
Bob Kaufman's vision was, it was in excellent taste, truly
cerebral, demanding constant attention to detail.
After studying Wilhelm Reich, I came to understand
that the Truth is bio-energetic, something profoundly
cataclysmic, it fluctuates but is congenial and suffuses learning
of the programmatic encounters of Mankind, and exists like
love standing up against a brick wall, there where the emotional
plaque may destroy it again and again... The tight-rope that
Bob wrote on was neither ethnic or poetic, it was simply chemical.
Yet, in the apocalypse of his brain, that stood for an era
long lost; that of dedication to Truth, that of seeing angels
on rooftops; and exclaiming with passion the words shaved
and carved like pencils into a pointed set of exclamations;
there was still the War of freedom verses sanctuary, not a
dramatic emblem, but a sign of deterioration, while the Times
change, and the phony sellers of phony truths get by,
and the interchangers of Freedom to Fear, tremble in their palaces
of greed and remorse, I remember living with him during the
eighty-four

democratic convention; we watched it on T.V., while Bob smoked
camels and shaking had nothing to say whatsoever about it.
   The Times
still change, and it seemed like the End of the World. But the
Times just got harder, and there was nobody really to talk to
about it. The yuppies were taking over everywhere, and
   my generation
was lost in a profound and dumb silence; swearing at the
crazy conventions of the age, staring down a dead end
without anyone to show them the way. This was when I found
you, you were sighing only a little too loud, you were
still angry, though unlike Kaufman, relatively healthy
and still powerful, that I thought that someone would
surely assassinate you, or kill you with pills and liquor
No, do not Shoot the Piano Player, not tonight anyways!
So Bob died of emphysema, I went north, gone crazy
by street life, and seeing white planes, ever so many
of them; while hiding out from the law. My first book was
published when I was eighteen and was entitled: *Night's Garden,*
then my second book was published when I was twenty-one
by Deep Forest Press, and it was called *Helen,* after a
friend of mine committed suicide in New York City,
by diving off a twenty-story building. I was published in
the Beatitude when I was nineteen, Clay Drum, and the Journal
of Contemporary Studies, and I studied Robert Duncan's
work. I practically lived in the Caffé Trieste. I knew Gregory
Corso, who to me was bigger than life. I also read the
Kabbalah, and was heavily influenced by French Surrealism
I was according to some an Enfant Terrible, but to some I was
just a scared kid who had lots of acne and never had any money
or place to live. I am twenty-eight now, and am alone, truly
alone, I walk the corridors and I carry with me your lyrics
from sixty-two to eighty-five, somehow they keep me alive, replacing
hell for heaven, thinking that some of us still bleed...
What is left of a man after he dies, but the symbols he dealt
with when he was living? Paul Landry, a good friend of mine,
just died of cancer last week. I have to say that he was truly
the best of the bunch, a printer, and a friend to the poets,
he was sensitive and kind, a rare combination. So this letter
may never reach you in person, but I know somewhere and somehow

we have a spiritual connection. I am writing to you to ease
the pain of being alone in this hospital. I hope you understand.
Well, I guess I've said enough for now. Will turn
on *Shot of Love* and listen to it again. God be on your side!!!

Love

Eric Walker
135 Johnson Lane
Carlotta, CA 95528
1/10/93

LETTER TO BOB DYLAN #2

DEAR BOB,

I'M LISTENING TO SHOT OF LOVE, AND I AM REACHING OUT
TO THE INNER CHILD THAT WROTE IT, THERE IS A VISION
SO VAST AND FULL OF CONSEQUENCES, THE MASTER'S HAND
IS ALSO GRACE AND COMPASSION; FOOD FED TO THE WORLD
THE VOICE OF LOVE ON THE PLANET. WORDS SAID, NUMBER
IN THE TIME THAT OUR VOICES DECAY. WE ARE PLANETARY HEROES,
AND O' GOD I NEED A SHOT OF LOVE. TOUR ALBUM IS DELICATE
AND PRECISE, EVERY GRAIN OF SAND IS NUMBERED, THERE IS
A BALANCE OF OPPOSITES, THAT SPECIAL TOUCH. THERE IS THE
EASTER VISION, THE PRECISE ROMANCE WITH CREATION. LOVE IS
ON OUR SHOULDERS. YOU MUST NOW REMOVE THE CLOAK OF DESPAIR,
YOU HAVING EVERYTHING. IN THE SORROW OF A NIGHT, I LISTEN
TO YOUR ALBUMS. THE BITTER DANCE OF LONELINESS IS THE STILLNESS
WITHIN THE VOICE. THE VOICE IS EVERYTHING. THE SPOKEN WORD
IS GOD, WE MUST MAKE TRANSVALUATIONS. SPEAK AND LISTEN.
I HOPE YOU READ THIS LETTER. COLUMBIA SHOULD TRANSMIT THIS
INFORMATION. HOPE YOU ARE WELL IN HEART.

LOVE, Eric Walker
(*A Beatitude Poet and a Friend of Bob Kaufman*).

LETTER TO WILLIAM EVERSON

Dear Bill-
I am happy! I am truly being productive. I have been both
writing and reading much. Am reading now *The Day On Fire*
by James Ramsey Ullman. It is a powerful book. I started
as a poet being friends with my master Rimbaud. It has
taken me far, and I learn from his pain, his tragedy. Genius
is the ultimate sky-god of the heart. I listen to the deep
roots of my own voice. I have finished publishing Notes
On A Surrealist and sending you a copy. I wish you a happy
birthday!!! I would like to come down around Christmas
time and visit you. Unfortunately I could not be at your
party this Saturday. How is Steve, love Steve very much
and it is my pleasure talking to both of you on the phone.
I think of Rimbaud a lot. He is on my brain, I am reading
some of the book everyday. His spirit was full of pain,
of frustration. To live such a frustrated life is difficult
to imagine. We must reconcile ourselves with the Land;
as poets we must feed our heads with prayer, absolve ourselves
in the nonconforming silence, that is ultimately what we
are. Like music we stop to say hello to our audience. Life
tends to greet us at every corner. I have never in my life
wholly stopped believing in Christ. God is everything
and is the conversation of Reality. To say the Supreme talks
through all matter, leading us back to Spirit. A conversation
with Rimbaud is interesting. I think a lot of what you said
to me about him. He stopped being his time and became another.
What we search for is eventually what we find. We will
Begin as infinite, only to last as long as the fields.
We tend the fields. We open them a new journey. I am
absolutely sure that we are creative sources thirsty for
the Light. To Become pure seer is to non-conform to your
time, to be the Future. A future dances in my heart, strives
to be different. I asked for my Birthday present: World
Peace. Now, just now, it seems to becoming a reality.
God has spoken through me, and I am part of the Salvation
of the Earth. Together then we must strive to be different.
The Superior Will is something other than strangeness.
Now is the Time that will make a difference. We stand at

a great vista, and can see ourselves reflected in the
mirror of yesterday. Tomorrow is still unpredictable. Poet
and poem are process, no more than the ether of Time. We
act, we make a decision to be, and we conform to that vision.
What's more, essentially we are perfect, to place the Creator
first is important. Now the Silence. The great Epoch of
Assassins.

Love Eric Walker 9/11/93

LIES

Tell us lies, for we do not want to hear the Truth!
Tell me lies for I can bear the wisdom of the ages,
besides I can't hear the names you call me!
I am all alone in the darkness of my head,
I am filthy with words I cannot make my own,
it's easier, more private this way,
I love the things that come from that place
we cannot speak of,
I am all alone,
tell me lies for I've forgotten my name,
and some call from the other side of morning,
I cannot pick up the pieces and I've gone
mad in my head, nameless are the ones
who travel from beyond the grave,
God why did you make this World full of hate,
I know somewhere is love,
tell me lies, caught in their dirty trap,
cold yellow sunlight,
it's a beautiful day after all.

LONELINESS

The World alone,
people alone, the Universe
spins in its egg of darkness,
everything is together but alone;
the blind-man in his black cage,
the baby and its cradle,
the cat asleep on your arm,
all the things alive experience loneliness.
I have lived amidst shadows for so long,
that the silence in my head beckons,
I have returned from the dead
to tell you living matters,
the woman on her mattress,
the naked song coming out of her throat,
speak but one word and I will be there,
the living shall know me as I know them,
and we will be alone,
in a room, an asylum, a church or cathedral,
a house beneath the ocean, a soft place in the earth,
and I shall follow you all your days,
till you hear me whispering in your ear
and as is dying so is life, the lonely day
fades into the light, and my heart quickens
to know someone else has actually felt me,
and in the wisdom of Death I know you
by the sound of your breath.

LOVE IS FREEDOM

To love something
is to free it of its chains,
a lame dog suddenly walks,
a bird caged begins to fly,
from this comes love,
to care for something
is to set it free,
for none of us can live in a cage,
so I set myself free,
I learn to divide and subtract,
I multiply my wealth
and the blood of my heart is strong,
pumping its red coins into the slot
of my heart, where activated
I become a camera,
taking pictures of the air,
and clouds disappear,
for I know how to love you,
and my beloved, I set you
free.

LOVE POEM FOR VAN GOGH

The masters hand is dark, untamed.
His eyes are wild, blue like rivers of the Seine.
Head absent one ear, and a face tanned lightly.
Haggard expression, almost tortured, slightly holy.
His stance is frail, body thin, like the wire of a statue
before the clay is laid into mold.
It's an unshaven face filled with fervor,
brightened by laughter and sublime tears.
The master's hand vivifies and gives dusk a hue all its own,
in new form on the canvas.
It describes the way a peasant walks after his work-day in the
    fields, and
how dusk shades him, so it hides his pallid lips,
and conceals their starved smile of poverty.
In these paintings there is no sign of madness, only clarity of
    vision, no
madman could paint with such grace or lucid colors!
You wear your visions on your hand like a glove
that fits its wearer tightly, stretched over loose skin.
The strokes half mad, seem wild but exact, tamed by fingers
    that claim
their mastery.
You alter the world with your brush; transform and move us
with its vision.
Your hand paints a window to all that it sees.
But there is not time for these visions in your asylum,
not when you lay sleeping with the knife at your side,
listening to the morning bells that call you to suicide.

LOVERS

The night is thick in our bodies,
junk taken from the rainbow's vein
hard heart trembling with droplets of champagne
I love you for hours
our sexes quiver like spiders dangling on a web
make sure the quickness of my love stays forever
thighs dancing with smooth bones clear as ice
in night's canyon we walk through shadows
and see mountains of mirror laid at our feet
in the valley of death we make our vows
in this temporary world we live for moments
that cease to exist long after death
I will remember your cool cap and gown
you wore your black necklace with its red ruby hour-glass
we drank all the scotch left in the fridge
from your lips I experienced madness
the kind that Luna gives
on the first day of Spring we gave to each other
the breath of love saying forever it will be
when the moment fades I still think back
to the time you held me so tight
when midnight collapsed.

LYING STILL

A weed rooted
in dirt, clumps
of bone buried
in central earth,
words bitten from
the hollow core,
stirring first,
hard hands felt knocking
at the door,
                    beat-red
                    his face breathing
                    a footstep of two
                    comes down to
                    the yellow brick;
remembering a time of innocence
like when I stayed at my grandparents
in the early summer, smell of air-ports
and fresh picked roses, the flat white
hand of an old woman dressing
the taut brown chicken skin,
basting it with butter and chives,
the ball-game on the set
and crimson candies laid in fine blue
ashtrays, a light at dusk against the badminton courts,
and the moon orange and looking
like a furious Eye in the fog,
and breakfast served up first
blink of the eye,
          other times when
          two fisted eyes
          shot me down
          from school corridors,
or the kidnapped swing
still flying free, unfurled
          before the invented
language took over,
before names spoke like bells,
and the silence of et cetera hummed

in my hand, when mom would stay home
from work because I had a bad fever,
      the extra languid day
      or two of absence,
the smell of pine
like a vitamin,
hiding in the ice-plant
      the deck warmed by the Sun
      soft-edged, glowing
old hidden graves
that I found concealed
in a grove of trees, pinned in
by the forest on all sides,
mysterious things,
              an old sun-tinted
              bottle dug up
              from our back yard,
              purplish fish of
              rainbow and
              glassy thread of night;
the ribs of a ghost
stick to my hand
like sand from the beach,
and the one-eyed gull diving head first
into water,
the cold splash before names
took resonance,
              the roar of jets
              lining the sky
              with thunderous meadows,
the weeping willow crying leaves
and scattering many tears
over the warm lawn,
              the gangs of kids
              scattering dirt and
              peeling oranges with
              clawed thumbs,
before the broken silences,
the heavy whistle of words sounding,
working their way into bone;

the warm heavy breath
sighing naked in a
cool green
the worm and the scorpion
with their tails curled,
the blue belly lizards scrambling
between the rocks,
  the pink dirt of
  Death Valley, and the
  warm chalky feeling of
  morning,
slippery feet in a bath-tub
brooding, her white webbed hands
that I met swimming
in the hotel pool of Kauai,
everyday, at almost the same time
for almost a week, then later
by mail, sunburnt back itching
with soft white flakes,
  before he hummed
  syntax slipped slowly
  into being,
the dragon-tail of the kite
turning figure-eights before the beach-sun
first long kiss like wet cotton
sticking to my mouth,
  before the blade
  heated in shadow
  cut smoothly,
smell of sea-air ionized in nostrils
and beach-rock sucking into skin,
  before the battle worn
  under celestial logic,
butterfly breaking into window.
horses tumbling with free & easy legs,
warm dawn hours of pink/blue velvet,
dirty bare-feet and toes squirming
under the dark sheet,
  before the wind torn
  from itself,

the tiger-eyed marbles spinning
freedom in the game,
the invisible old woman that lived in
my closet, involvement, the click
of bicycle tires, an oiled train engine,
humming bees, bricks built
of light & shadow, the still breathing
camera falling against the soft edges,
the icy fire of breath's geography
stopping short, lying still
beneath glass.

MASTER/TEACHER

Master/Teacher give me your hand
and let me follow
Time running its path
will not be here tomorrow
some children weep, some children laugh
take turns whittling life down to the marrow;
sing ghosts in the old house of a man put on trial
for no crime but insanity…
Open the door my lover and give me the key.
Learn to love in the open night
and to get right with the Light.
So Master/Teacher lend me your ear
and for the first time I will hear the words
together like a flock of birds
rhyming in the winter Sun.

MEMORIAL FOR MY STEP-BROTHER

Accident, shapeless the bullet of life traveled beneath
an artery for death, the fondness of broken sticks,
studying deer in the forest by the river signaling
back the death barked in you and made you bleed,
eye-level to the ground, what fatal wound crossed you
as you fed the hand-made tourniquet to some dying muscle,
born inside the night chatters of a listening banquet
of owls and bears, traveling like journeyman into the
outside of winter, crossing with a gun to the left shoulder,
tripping on stones, the redness of blood soaked into the ground…
Mystery, an endless pretense, a shy over-coming of death,
a predisposed virtue, as though inside the whole transposition
there is a corpse of rotting flesh.
This therapy of tears, welcomes the flood.

MONEY

God gave us the power to create
money hungry heaven waits
on earth as it is....

Walking down the street,
looking for an easy fix,
hoping that there is no slick way
to fall like that,
on one's knees,
heaven help us, please!

Capitalism sucks,
good luck is having not to worry
where you lay down
your weary head,
hobo dreams
of the far-out future,
look back then forward,
God loves those who dream....

Lonely God, in his lonely reality,
spend time making time tick in a torn up way
looking for the good, buy our new tasty tit,
suck, sip, savor, the thing is real, by God!
look for happiness but find shit shapeless
shopping malls of silent decay,
look for our new buy if you can jar of spam,
our perfect tasteless pork-chops,
look for an angry jump
it's just a jolly hump,
a human hand, there is a curse upon the land,
money, money, sweeter than honey,
how it cures our blues,
either way you lose.

MORNING

Precise, the logic of mirrors,
the fantasy begins and ends here,
we bring flowers for the god of morning,
winter has come, there is frost on the earth,
there languished in the silence
is a man with a broken tongue;
vanish, hide from me,
turn your deaf ear on the broken wind,
star that turns in you,
morning and the coming day relaxes,
set free.

MUSIC LADY

Together the warm play
of images, patterns musical
notations, realized feelings,
such and such in the stoned illusion
of tomorrow, we discuss Dylan and Tim Buckley,
we rant against the sorrows of people not in tune,
ages in our eyes, sweet kiss upon the forehead,
smiling depth of your poetic voice,
she singing and playing, she the guitar
of the moon shaped like a crescent of steel chords,
stood upon the shadow of her bed, warmth wrapped
in quiet and meditating hugs, long eyes with
the sweat of love, she dancing, tunes and worlds
of air in her quiet meandering, she the tonal rainbow
of earth and sun, the sky-Father has met in us,
has tuned our instruments in compassion for one another,
rock of ages, mysterious woman with music as a child
of wonder, turning to the wind for comfort;
shy cat of loose change, eyes dancing with images
of love, a slow train of instruments charges through
your living-room, as I toast you with red wine,
meandering on your carpet of tomorrow.

NATURE'S WAY

The ecology of dreams
makes splendid icons,
God made everything with variety,
his original signature is on all of Creation,
the silent planet weeps for the hidden Sun,
the air is blue, the footsteps of Man are scarlet with
tinges of dark green,
the color of decayed money,
we exist for one reason: to take inventory of the
beauty God gave us, the children play in the fields,
kites fly high in the sky,
it is Nature's way to see these things,
in the unheard forest the axe cracks
and splinters fall,
the tree is silent because no one hears it,
another vote is cast through the deaf winter,
the spotted owl has migrated to heaven,
the stars cold and icy look down upon us,
Nature is waiting for the sound of shattered glass,
it is the mirror of God that has cracked,
the ocean cold as snow boils over,
the green planet is in a house with no windows,
the animals suffer in silence,
greed has broken out,
but the river is flowing red with blood,
peace on Earth for all creatures,
alive and still in the plant's womb.

NEVER BORN

As though the endless Summer never happened,
eyes did not see the painted flesh
moving in rhythm to the sea,
changing time took no notice
of the bright pennies thrown in a stalwart fountain
where disease and beauty grapple as if in love-play,
the dancers did no dances, no eyes watched them,
the sky was neither liquid nor full of colored balloons,
nothing took place, no air in lungs,
no heart-beat shaped itself out of a black tube,
no brain mimicked its coughing light,
nobody saw the bent and forked highway
from which nothing was born, nothing promised,
nobody felt the Life that did not happen,
and nobody worried that it would be to blame,
never born, never conceived, only the rocky ocean
could feel its tiny embryo dance a little before
it vanished, like a pebble unimagined forever caught
in its calloused machine a cog of Faith from which
we master our birth, only once upon a time something turned
its head towards the womb, drying its eyes beneath the
heavy plates of skin, never to return again.

NEW YEAR

Brother year you have passed
into darkness like the others,
now this infant year is taking your place,
a fanfare from yesteryear's broken night
has been placed into my empty hands,
I do not fear the coming of morning
sleeping with the inhabitants of
an insane-asylum, I just miss my cappuccino
and smoke-dreams, dried eyes mock my presence,
feeling underhanded I walk to the hospital-café
and pick myself up with some coffee,
behind the make-up there is some secret spice
that we wear to keep our hair from falling out,
dreams are for free, war is tantamount in the struggle
for survival, World Peace so cold in the night
where white men walk amidst black skeletons
who dream of appetites that can only fail
to provide the bread to the children of starvation,
there is only the midnight of doubt that breathes
like fog on the mirror, windows wet with rain
and the fat arm of the law dances next to the
maddening sleet of yesterday, how many bombs
will we manufacture in the coming year while schools
go bankrupt and a new president weeps in white walled
rooms and on ticker-tape parades? He speaks on T.V.
of the end of the World, seven years of plague pursue
the time-infested century, but the love of warm places
has handed me this bed,
where the screams of mental patients dwell
in the broken air of mindless décor,
dream of a vein where blood trembles like gold,
of a cigarette that is never lit but is always smoking,
of a coke machine that is for free, of a dozen quarters
that the reek in your fist, of glasses and cups full of coffee
and wine, of salesmen who sell computers to the blind
of shipless waves forever diaphanous and green,
of what conquers in the midsummer dream of houses
and bars, and counterpart, a year to dream them in,

smiles and components of smiling faces,
yes a year died last night only to give birth to another
while what is lasting has come crazily yelling its
open armed dance with the skeletal reams of paper
tonnage, only to sleep again with nude and glowing
fingers rapping on some table-top where magicians
play for free, hiding on secret glance of their lover's
daughter, new-born and happy to see the glare of yesterday
in a newly lit room where the voices linger, and smoke
and candles bleed against the windy surface of
God's Calendar, Happy New Year! I say while
the asylum is drained of laughter, swimming in a
precious wind of doubt and hapless stares of fomenting
eyes so stiff and white that nobody knows who will turn
the water to wine and who will survive the wind of the night.

1/01/1993

ON THE EVE OF MY 29TH BIRTHDAY

I have been assessing myself,
my craft is fine-tuned, my eye-sight clear,
my love spans the whole earth, my muse is silence
carved into a tree of words, I have been an alchemist
perfecting the dross, tired in flames of self-suffocating madness,
I have returned from the Dead, I am a visionary
and a lover of LIFE, I love my life it is mine
and I take care of it.
Tonight I kissed a girl, it made me happy,
a long hug from a friend and some birthday presents
over a hot cup of coffee.
We spoke of our fears, our longings
I am a man, not a boy!
I grow into age like a distant heat shimmering mirror;
her kiss lingers, I am hers!
I fall on my knees thanking God for my new life,
I love the objects of beauty, I am longing for a new
friendship, her eyes held mine, long hugs are good,
I feel growing tension of my heart, strung like a bow...
I am following the North Star, I am a poet and I am a seeker
of Truth, there is only poetry and LIFE, the two are
both in Union now, I sleep into my twenty-ninth year,
tomorrow will be my birthday, and now I am up thinking
about this thick age, these traversing silences
that echo in midnight calls, like old Dylan songs
performed on a piano with ghost fingers,
I am with the Light, positive and shinning all night long.

ON THE ROAD

How times have changed
since you came walking these streets,
looking at dirty America;
awakening the angel,
and sleeping in wet beds
with sheets smooth as snow,
hot and cold in your brandy throats...
Oh I tell you times have changed
it is a different place,
the pigeons in the park are all grey
and luke-warm bodies,
and the brandy is tasteless.

PEARL

Iridescent granule
of perfect transcendence;
child of the black bright bonanza
of silent irrigation;
formed years of smiling flesh
kept in the soft dark gut;
shell bent muscle spent,
a pejorative knife to cut deep
the natal head; precious cool
saliva of nature's soft eye;
unusual occurrence, pressured
by the quietude of nauseous undertakings,
of a liquid coffin spills its quick aqua heart;
Poem from the sea with its
academic thrills; a thorn of light
weeping to be set free; a titanic
birth carves its jet white wonder;
seed that belongs to the Poet's
labor, caught like a star opened
from beneath the sea's unconscious
desire.

PEN DREAMS

Ink and pen dare to write
and as the writer sets it upon the shelf at night,
it begins to sprout though the harsh dirt of reality
as silently as the sands of time begin to fall.
And as the child begins to dream,
the livers of illusion are redeemed.
The reality is once again set,
and upon it are the lost dreams of the creators,
but as the plant does die and the seeds do root,
as astute as the writer, the imagination still remains more astute.
So the pen becomes the creator, the paper time, and the words
of dreams.
The illusion is set, the cycle is completed.

POEM FOR JESSE

Go Jackson, go!
Come to see the children play
they wait for you all day
in South Africa they raise their slanted faces
they are mothers and creeds of all races
in America we wait out the Reagan years
carrying Reagan cheese from free bins of the unemployed
America, the kingdom, the race in rafters and peoples
the naked and the annoyed
our Anthem is with you
our children wait in the door way of their youth
the day stands guard
there is melted cheese on the campaign booth
there are posters and names called
the hinges are all rusty at the handles
Americans strong labor, movement aroused in rusty gears
solid motion taking place
and the children in the river of industry drown
and I'm unemployed and from a small town
where labor consist of cutting down trees all day
and the workers only care about their pay
the Sunrises in the redwood memorial park are beautiful
especially with the graves of soldiers carved out in shiny marble
remind us of Vietnam and passed loved ones,
...in the school yard the children are playing leapfrog, their hands
rise gently back and forth, watch the pendulum go
swing gently in the air, touch soon the moon and dance
go Jackson, go!

PORTRAIT OF HELEN KAY (1966-1985)

She had her golden dress on, she was barefoot walking across
Telegraph, she was small, brown-eyed, and had short brown hair.
She was a peaceable spirit, one small fragile woman in a large
and frightening world. Not too many of us remember her now,
  there's me
I remember her because I truly loved her, and there's black Bert
who I haven't seen for quite awhile, he remembers her too.
But just the same she was a rememberable person, a shape and
a sound so new and unused, the at the same time with a certain
poise that resounds in the wind, a graceful experience that most
likely died with her. She was wild, and her eyes shot forth in
the darkness, staring at everything, curious as a kitten. She was
soft and emotional, the kind of person who did not stand pressure
that well. The woman mirrors the child, the child dreams of
becoming a woman, and the two meet in adolescence. Time
  kills dreams
destroys their fragrance, unchastens womanhood, brings life to a
halting stop. The dreams drop like stones in a pool of tears,
and the cool insignia of reality takes over, makes present everywhere
its taste and flavor, that forbids the sanity of a young girl
to escape, and forces her to turn against her dreams. Helen looked
to the future, but mirrored the present with the grace of a deer,
leaping over the abyss. Helen was special, unique, different.
She had a great sadness, a great loneliness, an overwhelming cause
of disbelief fighting a great wonder and a beautiful innocence.
Like the time she dissected a dead sparrow she had found on the
sidewalk; first she took it up on the roof of a house, sat down and
cut it open with her pocket knife. She told me she loved heights,
the higher the better. It was not fate that she died nor accident,
it was self-willed. The force of her life and the vitality of death
sometime in her ascent encountered each other with the trembling
beauty of blood driven against snowy pavement.
A shy creature controlling her madness and her beauty
with bright flames that nobody seemed to see.
Now long after I think about it, I barely recognized, or
I didn't know what they were, but they were flames, and she was
burning alive. Sad eyes, pouting in the corner with her white rat
climbing her olive colored hands. Then the burst, the shouting,

throwing my possessions out her dorm window, angry, hitting me
with her fist; the negative side of love. And the fury of Life
resounding in her, upsetting the system with its pounding anxiety,
knowing something's wrong but not being able to do anything about it.
She was not satisfied with being a student and she did not take the
student life as seriously as she wanted to. She found that life
was more or less a pattern of thoughts that grew inside her;
blossoming in her troubled psyche. Great thoughts make martyrs of
us all; the sounding of darkness on light, the playful creativity
that is suppressed, and then realized again, can kill a thousand
ghosts in war of fragments shot into the window of Time. The life
of Helen was short, it was full of awful feelings, but had a great
tenacity. Such a body full of sweetness that must of fell through
gray clouds, dying on the street, around Christmas, she jumped off
a twenty story building, to die, to be gone, no longer surrounded
by the charms of childhood; a true woman's death, dead and broken
on the pavement. Sometimes I ask myself how badly did it hurt, then
I remember her sweetness, her playfulness, and her body warm and
fertile with life. Death is hard to take, especially if it is somebody's
death that you loved dearly, and is not a statistic on the evening news.
Bright eyed and full of emotions, that is the way I chose to remember
her. A celebration, a true lover, with lips of pious judgment.
The truth died with her, the sad loving sweetness of a body that
possessed life, of an open heart that screamed in the darkness.
What I wonder is that if she had made the choice to kill herself,
what happened to that life-force inside her, what changed her
to force upon her an unhappy death, what made that freedom
dissolve that she loved so well??? According to her boy-friend in
New York City, she took off all of her clothes and found a building,
climbed it somehow without the police arresting her, of course
the police were busy arresting everybody else, and jumped from
the tall building naked. Yet she went in her birthday suit, she
died with freedom, freedom she chose along with the death that
belonged to her. And here's the song: Blood Sweat and Tears, and I'm
listening to it right now: "God bless the Child that got his own",
this is what she could not get her own, but maybe she already had
what she was looking for; tears empty and dried like blood,
tears so long afterwards, a crust of bread, a child's longing as
the end of our childhoods mixed, mingled and said goodbye together.
Washed in the river of blood, I felt sadness and anger that she

could not feel any longer, that sadness was her grace, and I still
feel it today; the longing for lost childhood, the sense of magic
long dead and forgotten, still preserved in my heart. Now she is a
forgotten, a fact hazy and simplified by death, never to be reversed.
I remember the drawings of hers that I burned, that were pencil
people screwed into paper, tortured by soundless screams,
as though ashes were not enough, and I burned them in the fire,
watching them blacken and leave this world, perhaps to mingle with
her ashes. Where, in the flowers of execution, in the blind portholes
of a ship made strictly of rose-buds, in the crackling wire of
electricity, in the shy significance of dancing between flames,
or in the earth, spread like a river of memories, oh where do you
exist??? Let flowers pour over your death, aimless and searching
for the pain of your ghost, tear-drops falling into the sea,
remembering all the words you said, and the poems I tore up in front
of you, the ones I can't rewrite, a celebration of death and life,
in one instant, taking from you the things that are of importance
to the parade that never ends; more flowers for the awakening of your
emotions from beyond the grave, a ghost caught in memory of life
I cannot possess, a love-song wild and free, a simple fawn born again
in the relaxing silence of birthing blood, a raging fire wild and
out of control, a service held in your memory everyday at the
birth of the Sun... Memories are selective, and the ghost that lives
in us is still alive, pounding at our chest. I live everyday in
reminder of her life cut short at nineteen, and wondering what would
of become of her if she had lived. I dreamed that she turned into a
snow-flake in one crazy moment stained with blood. And no
heaven-ward she climbed back up to the sky to come down as rain
and sunshine. Helen, wherever you are I still love you, and in my
silent raisin, I plant a seed shriveled by Sun.
Goodbye childhood, the woman has Come!

08-09-1991

PROPHETS OF MCDONALD'S

The Christ has come.
I found him in McDonald's, eating a Big Mac
on fast, a quarter pounder.
His address is 102 Mount Ararat, Apt B.
His sermons consist of where to buy a pot roast for $1.00.
He brings us good news.
Campbell's soups have gone down 10 cents.
He says he is his own boss,
but I think he really works for Safeway.

RATIO OF WARMTH

The moon sometimes wraps
around me on nights
when the ants are cold,
its fires burn bodily into
my brows, as the naked
and dead pass,
growing hungry and cold
inside their brains,
my back is filled with
whiteness of your wide-eyed
troubles, tasting me in
this dark greenery of air.

REALITY ON A DOORSTEP

Headline – "Bush Takes Stand".
Cold, foggy mornings, only catching a glimpse
of what's inside,
Throwing typewriter spitted, copied, pressed paper –
Rubberbands rolled neatly in a stack.
Reading "Peanuts" on a cold, Sunday morning –
but I haven't the time.
Compressed propaganda rolled up with a ribbon on it.
Smiling faces of instant joy. "Have a nice Day"-
how many times have I said that - sixty or more.
Hard paved cement forsaken by all cars.
Me, caped with the millstone of reality.
Redeeming phone calls – store bought forgiveness.
Rubberbands flying off in all directions
leaving the reality to unravel.
Cursing under my breath, yawning for my bed, asking,
"Why did I ever begin?"

February 25, 1989

REASON AND GOD

Rhetoric fills the shelves of libraries,
the kind master resumes his handiwork,
stretchers of unwritten pages scuttle in tiny
rooms that shine like dew-drops in the Sun,
ages write their handsome blood in silent apertures
changed from the furious dark;
masters accomplished in the brooding tides
of Unconscious wonder search their white hairs
for a finality like a summit of chairs hidden in
a clean fortress of clouds...
We reason out our search for quietude, but there is
the simple kindness that overstretches everything,
like a vast funeral of unseen light.

REFLECTIONS OF PARADISE

Infinite nature, resounding like the sea.
The serenity of this place, where things grow
Like wild fire, reaching the endless Universe.
A tree that stretches out beyond the known cycle,
into the rhythms of mountains, rooted beneath Christ's eye.
The thing that never ends, celestial coming of warmth
in the icy dream of Salvation.
And the woman who changes her face to be a smiling angel
of life, life given over to life, created long ago.
In that creation could linger like this, in the form of
smooth stones, polished by the endless river.
Reflections of reflections.
A billion Suns wrapped in a gold band, glittering on her finger.
Mountains unlike any mountains you have ever seen.
And valleys greener than the greenest thing.
Perfect virgin forest, uncut and unlogged.
When does this end, you ask?
When forever melts into dusk.
When time goes backwards.
When she turns ugly, who is infinitely beautiful.
When the spider unweaves its web.
When the solid mountain melts like ice.
This endless sea churning blood.
A trillion more Suns reflect in the night sky.
Paradise perfect, like the marriage feast of two gods.
Broken mirror, man in his solitude cannot see.
There, where the root clasps of the mountain, a perfect
reflection of infinity.

RELEASE

The day is spent in anticipation
then final climax, the old hospital walls
are no more a vista, but only the distant memory
of glue upon the razor skin,
release into the community, happy thoughts
bubbling in my head, I walk downtown to cash
my check, the discomfort of being locked down
is a dim reminder of something very sad,
I return to my new home victorious with a pack of
Camels and a brand new lighter, I touch ground,
seething with free hands typing at the void,
sunlight is carefully filtered through the shades on
my window, I dance with laughter,
the sea of madness quaking in my guts is gone,
the ugly torment has settled,
I sit down to write a poem, the only thoughts
that come to my head are: come and go into
the new day with a greater hope, for now I am
free to walk the streets, no longer a mad-man in
a haggard jacket, but a truth-seeker inside a rainbow
of glittering gems, this I know, after the release
some hours ago.

REMEMBER WE'RE PEOPLE

The loose sky
throws down its spare change;
laughter cries at the doors of the hospital,
like a camera it burns into the walls and
the eyes of the patients broken by love
and made chaste by hate, human all too human
brought under fire by a cheating mind,
the twisted day sings of its slaughter,
chanting the wind blows the ashes off the stone plaza,
white chairs and blue pajamas,
the shouting of skulls broken in the shame and ridicule
of inhuman silence,
do we cast eyes off a glance, and do we belong
locked up like this?
The secret dancers aspire to tap dance with the wind,
summer casts blue into cold gray, habits are hard
to break, the hammering continues,
through the scared light there comes dreaming,
to sleep and forget the dry stucco walls and the fence
that has been climbed and will be climbed again…
Resonance on a highway of bodies claps its hands
and crumbles into air, there is the taste of cleaned
brick that tumbles into washed yellow floors that are
danced upon by humpbacks and strangers, not a road,
but a glued surface, like a giant stamp placed mid-way
between heaven and hell; some throw milk on the floor when
they get angry, or a whole plate of peas,
tossup lunch and go for a stroll,
remember who we are, and like you we fall into our
crumbling minds, blessed like murder, or love,
just a challenge from the weary beneath your footsteps.

REMEMBERING THE DEAD

In my life I have known people
who have died;
I have seen the ancient rain
of Bob Kaufman perish,
I have known a young woman
who jumped off a building,
killing herself on the snowy
streets of New York City,
I have loved animals,
I have written epitaphs
for those who could not make it,
I have known a man who lived to be
eighty-eight years old,
he talked much about his life,
and I learned from him the art of poetry,
today we mourn the dead,
we say hello to the graves of the unborn,
we cherish the magic of their lives
when they were with us,
and knowing that they were taken
makes us believe that we too will be chosen
to leave fatefully on a day in an hour
behind the loved ones that we care for,
and we will be mourned like those before us,
in requiem the dead walk on air,
the light does not go out,
but burns forever,
into the night we go gently
like lovers
who rest peacefully on their beds,
entangled in each other's arms,
laid forever to rest.

SAYING GOODBYE

The children of darkness bend their naked arms
I ask for a cigarette
and leave you in the kitchen without a hug,
I hope for something that I cannot possibly
accomplish, lighting my cigarette
in the silence of your forehead,
I ate the body and dreamed of the ghost
sucking down the last of your tobacco,
my eyes bent like a spoon around
the kitchen table
where I charged all night like a ram
with broken horns, my dreams mumbling
into sleepy dark air,
I blinked my eyes and steered down
the stair, boarding red car with
stony windows, I watched you turn
from me.

SIXTEEN YEARS

Since last seeing you,
the star in your flesh burned,
the child of night conformed
to an image of solitude,
too young, far too young,
majesty in broken arrows of innocence,
buried beneath a heart-shaped tattoo,
a tree of light & shadow beats with every breath
you take, with every whispered word you make,
a strong resilience, a Sun in chains,
mountain laurel and rolling rocks, she's
begging to know, nobody sleep in that village
where your hair bleeds, wind upon the city,
eyeless gods coming from down beneath the roots
of networking redwoods, peaceful dove sleep deep,
my knowledge is fastened to your innocence,
a precarious station where beggars walk
in mirrored hallways, and the Unicorn
white as a manger talks of the stars in giving
her magic, her maiden-head, to the coming Dawn.

who had just bought them a round of
drinks while Rebecca had shared her change
to play the jukebox, I turned the brier
musical histories to find Dylan's Jokerman,
I played it, and as it came on I could
feel the beer, it was as though a cleansing
was taking place, and outside the ghosts
awaited us, piling lumber and steel gates
so high that one would swear the sky
was melting, and the moon was a soft
disk of flesh and blood. His birthday
a gate into that silent No Man's Land
forayed south of the great salty lakes.

　　　The night wind played in the streets,
as he climbed the stairs of the building
he could hear Jenny & Rebecca talking to
somebody. As he opened the door he could
see for himself a man sitting at the
kitchen table looking like some perfect
stranger. Indeed he was, though one of
Rebecca's close friends, he had arrived
on the Greyhound from Boston. Up until
then he had shared Rebecca and Jenny
with no one. The night dissolved its windy
fortress. He was walking poems in pocket,
he was walking to a bar where he intended
to read his poems. It was poetry night at
the green-light, and yes, as the wind drew
dark clouds from the east, he entered
the bar, carrying his books of poems.
He sat down and waited for the show to
begin. Soon he was sitting in a crowd of
people that looked like they came from
all walks of life, not your usual bar crowd,
but an almost romantic affection drove
them together here, away from those
dark & windy streets, here in the warmth
of the Green Light, the power of the
word was sharpened like glass upon glass,

and as I sat I watched them pass the
'open' list around, a ritual I had participated
much in. There was a four-year old girl
sitting next to me, biting a necklace of
amber-green plastic beads, her name was
Sarah, and somehow shared the scat with
all little girls I had ever met, including Cedar,
the child with her green berries spilling
from her golden basket, Cedar who I
thought of constantly, who I had listened
to the stair way to Heaven while crossing the Mississippi,
who someday I would return to, and rest
with on a sunny day, rest from all the games
Children play.

When one applauds after someone reads
a poem what actually are they saying? Comfort
in the Night full of clouds, execution or silence
smooth voice running over the dead ears
of a private synagogue of culture, language
cut into glass dolls forms a perfect paper-weight,
to hold down the heart in its trembling fury.
People should really hold hands at poetry
readings, pretending they are trapped in
a cave, listening only to the sliding whispers
of stone creaking below them, only the air
sparkling with rivulets of water mixed in the
deep unknown of ash and clay. And the
Poet is the singular 'I' pressed upon the
darkness like a trembling light that could
set them free. A man invests in a piece of
property, he spends his life savings on it,
he must work like a slave the rest of his
life just to possess it; every morning when
he wakes up before coffee or shower or shave
he looks at the deed of the land, and dreams
of retiring and building a large house on it.
But for now he must work for a living. We
ignore the Poet's dreams as we ignore our
own lives. We are possessed by the future
but must work hard to live in the present.

We became our own nomenclature; names,
personal histories, all raise-eyed staring at
us in the darkness like a heap of corpses.
Somebody's finger is pointing at us, somebody's
hand is busy autographing a poem. A man with
silver hair laughs like a devil. Another
jazz musician chases down his vodka like Faust.
The man with the ultimate warrior jacket
turns for a profile while children of beauty
step off the bus and gather in a garden of
white terraces. There is a warm sound in
the winter night crumbling like snow off
the mountain. She sleeps, on her stomach while
I draw butterflies tattooed like wind upon
her back. I draw sleeping giants on the living
room floor. The Windy city. Sleep without
placement, light without shadow. And little
Sarah as I finish reading my poems, smiles
with a certain sophistication that only children
know about while biting down on her green
beads.

    I left Chicago one day with my box of
Wilderness. My books and gag and weapon all
traveled with me. I slept on the Greyhound,
my dreams like bad coffee brewed in my head.
I left my body one morning in Idaho. I
went through the Eye of the Sun, to the
other side of morning. Drums played and sin
smelled of burning flesh. The towns I had
visited in the night were all decayed with
orange rust and silver flames. Soon I was
made into a tiger pacing in a cage of
time, in the solar flight of madness and
the slicing of heat upon my hands
woke me with a disturbing gulp of flesh. I
saw little Daniel asleep in his mother's lap
like Christ & The Virgin Mary, his black skin
shiny like a coffee bean. I cried that morning
as we waited in Reno, refueling for gas.

THANKSGIVING

Giving grace in the asylum,
residents receive dinner seated
at tables with rich food,
there is a tentative smile
in your face, and a loving door
opens somewhere in the back-room,
I contemplate the turkey meat that
is fresh and white cooked poultry
of the living family,
and freedom of those who
walk in chains become the satisfied
and dreaming celluloid of a new wisdom,
bare skin on patterns of snow,
dreamy eyed and speaking in songs
of heart-felt memories,
the holidays of depression
resume their coming fever,
sky-scrapers of comfort
rise in our throats,
and the coffee tastes good
with cream and sugar,
asleep a dozen times and restful
blue that shouts in our skin,
alive in the distance, giving
thanks to God with small fingers
probing the secret fold of parted
waters.

THINGS TO REMEMBER

Under the Volcano Malcolm Lowry
Dark is the Grave Wherein My Friend is Laid-Malcolm Lowry
Season in Hell (Rimbaud)
Theatre & Its Double Artaud
Goethe: The Sorrows of Young Werther
Hyperion Holderlin
Marat/Sade Peter Weiss
The Infernal Machine Jean Cocteau
The Day on Fire James Ramsey Ullman (first book that
    interested me, read it at 14).
Jung Dreams Memories and Reflections
Paul Claudel Break of Noon
Andre Gide The Immoralist
Andre Malraux Man's Fate
Ariel Silvia Plath
Time of The Assassins Henry Miller
Under the Sign of Saturn Susan Sontag
Van Gogh: The Man Suicided by Society Antonin Artaud
Zohar: Moses De León

THROUGH THE DAY

I get high with a little help from my friends
and listen to Beatle songs played on the radio
living on the fringe sometimes is fun
but usually it's the edge of another reality
that stumbles and catches you off your guard
California is the place to go when you need to
forget how fucked the world can be
it's my native country
so fast it has grown
through the day it has become a giant
tied down by the little people
staked at the earth like some Gulliver
whose travels have lead him to the twentieth century
the country is a giant held captive
by the little people who make it work all day
feasting on the plentiful bones of those who've died
skeletons of the earth crawl out
and revoke the day with orders of I must live
and to die is something important
and Gulliver shakes his fingers
and the tiny threads are broken
and the giant rages at the toil
of these small people
who carry off bread with the breath of life leaking
through them and the sky crawls to be born again
and the Sun burns its hot tobacco
smoking heat in the living room
and the giant sits down to dinner
and gorges himself to a fine feast
and the coldness of winter hides everything from us
through the day we see blind
tears of suffering children are better left
unmasked.

THROUGH THE NIGHT

These are celebrations,
this naked time is a rebirth of darkness,
following the dawn we walk on water's edge,
taken aback by the green fountain,
like a wet horse I ride you
through the faithful light,
imaginings of sweet cedar
like ointment poured upon our heads,
in this bed I sleep alone
crying tears of salt,
men's blood mixes with mine,
this vascular earth is a symphony of blind cells,
the light cuts just like a razor,
beneath this canopy of stars
I see your eyes,
a ghost of the dead walks in innocence,
knowing you from the time you were young.

TIME

How quickly years pass,
how slowly Time trickles
from sorrow to joy, like snow
melting off a mountain...
The fruit ripens, drips from the vine...
In the mirror we see the perpetual performances
of actors missing their cues...
It is dark sojourn through the blind window
where dusk veils her angelic arms and casts
her legs like dolphins on the sea...
Orange-yellow, the hypnotic light of a dying Sun,
the equinox of moon on water...
Time cuts its way through the skin; the emotional
climax of lovers, the sad faced saviors broken
on clock's arms...
In lunar silences we see and believe that love
is magic predisposed by charity...
Amidst laughter and tears
Time leads us through decades,
and spends our youth like coins for the dead.

TOO PERSONAL

SOME POETS SAVE THEIR WORK FOR AFTER THEIR DEATH,
A POST-MORTEM RECLUSIVENESS OF THE STANDARD JOY
WE ALL LIVE BY, NICOTINE DREAMS BLOW INTO SILENT
SMOKE-RINGS THAT SLIP UPWARDS, THAT WEDDING OF BLOOD
BROUGHT ON BY THE REFUSAL TO SHARE, AND WHO IS TOO DISTANT
THAT FARAWAY GOD THAT TREMBLES AND EMBRACES EVERYTHING?
TOO PERSONAL, MY GIRLFRIEND LEFT ME, I AM ALONE, I WAS
AN ABUSED CHILD, I WANT THE SEXUAL DARKNESS TO ENTER
AND SWALLOW ME, I BELONG TO KNOW ONE, I HAVE HALLUCINATIONS,
I AM PREGNANT WITH MY FATHER'S CHILD, I WANT NO ONE TO HEAR
THIS, I CANNOT RISK MY PRIVACY.
YET SOME KNOW THE SPIRIT TO BE TOO CLOSE,
THE WANTING WORDS FLOW ONLY WHEN THEY ARE ALONE,
POETS LIKE MAGICIANS MUST NEVER GIVE AWAY THEIR SECRETS,
LIKE THE WOMAN IN HER PRIVYS WRITING POEMS TO A BOY-FRIEND
THAT ABANDONED HER, OR A FATHER WHO RAISED HIS SON ONLY
TO KNOW THAT HE WAS A WORKING-CLASS STIFF AND NOT A POET.
NO! THESE WORDS ARE UNIVERSAL, SUPERNATURAL, A WINDOW
TO THE FUTURE AND TO ALL THAT BELONG THERE.
WE CANNOT WIPE THE SURFACE SO CLEAN THAT THE MARBLE
WILL NOT SHINE. WE MUST INVENT LIVES TO OUR HEAD
TO BELONG AGAIN TO OUR DEATHS THAT ARE A CERTAIN INVASION
TO OUR PRIVACY.

TREATING THE MENTALLY ILL

Standing ground,
Not letting them get to you,
Pushing them away,
Where is the warmth?
In the conference room we meet
every morning to talk about our problems,
recluse, refusal to lift this heavy weight,
I'm ill, who has done this to me?
Creative despondency, loosing my religion,
Talking to Christ on the big phone,
Answering voices that answer to me only,
chill out; reward avarice.
The tortured routine of looking into the mirror,
the weary battle with nurses probing, searching
you for contraband, the crazy lights sucked into
a cavern of noise, an endless duty to wake up
for medication, to sleep in sullen dreams of 'why
cannot I escape?' or the pressured silence
that rings in your ears, a cage.
Looking, seeing him lift into the program, that he or
she is not beautiful, but teeth decay, not collected
but fragmented, not real but reluctant, testing
and trying to dig into a black hole, is there anything there?
Get up! Respond! Take you out, then put you back in,
reason fails, but life is a compromise, I mean get real,
self-devaluation, self esteem is a profit off the beautiful
and wreckless spirit of destruction, atom bombs, weird but
familiar animalization, brought by suffocating redemption,
get real or pay the price!
Standard modification. Love America!!!
Treat yourself to a friendship hug, loss of hope,
Self doubting, be real, the frenzy of air moving from
room to room, crazy-talk, self-reflective treatment into
the abyss, refined manners of Adam & Eve in a circus tent;
tornados of human pride sweep these hospital bare-walled,
crumbling egos, egoless and wise with wanton fear. Get real!

TROUBLE

There in the sanction of freeways
God bent reclusively over a giant mirage,
spent reflections on the ugly cancer
of Life's forest, Man entered to cut
down the sea of green, great machines
to destroy the blind wood of a thousand years,
now night stares into its lonely pit,
now God dreams of his green fingers,
the blood flows from one point to another;
White Man plays God inside the mausoleum of sleep,
conquers the Spirit with the under-rating of inventions
that heal only the rich and healthy lepers of the new
social caste, a Western metaphor for the lower class
deprived bellies of starvation,
enter Satan in his white space-ship,
mirrors heaven with an ageless stare,
burns down the factories of light with black
madonnas who hide in a furnace of blinding decay,
they feed us medicine to kill the God inside us,
pills to comfort our ills, purity masked with freedom,
the nude crazed dream of another's sleep,
there is trouble in the mountain, trouble upon the rock,
where rests the double-light of a thousand eyes
too blind to see.

TRUTH

Told about the mysterious seed
called Truth.
It is a tree filled with fruit
that never falls on hard ground.
It is most definitely something relative
to itself, though I've heard the truth told
on many a full moon, and the fury we have
divides the truth into two particles.
Words resonant with words, where is this going?
Questions revolve with questions, and Time lapses
in the asking.
Where do I go from here?
The animals know Truth by its smell;
they'll eat it if it smells good.
Seen but never identified, always disguised
in the garb of the street, I see Truth walking
by me, only you can tell by its hipster walk
that it's Truth disguised as Truth.
Hypnosis, we are hypnotized to believe in the truth
of dictators.
Many small truths make up one big Truth.
Lies, all lies told by men to enslave men.
I am a slave to the truth.
Amidst the ladder of solitude I find it told to me
in the coldest hour.
Truth made by itself, self-created.
Never tell lies in the face of Truth.
Truth swallows you, and you allow it to engulf your
every day.
Truth loves fiction.
Justice is done only in the nick of Time.
Truth saves!
Think Truth everyday, spending time to reflect
on how different we are, like every apple in that Tree.

UNDER THE INFLUENCE
(AN UNOFFICIAL HISTORY OF ROCK-N-ROLL)

Every morning I listen to classic rock. It begins as early as
seven and ends sometimes past midnight. Sometimes I blare
it, sometimes I like it soft. It casts a spell on me. The lyrics,
I'm a lyric junkie, like Pink Floyd's Animals, or Jim Morrison's
Waiting for the Sun. I especially like the Velvet Underground.
Good down and dirty realism of the Sun in incognito, of
the blast of heat coming from cool town with loving hand
searching and baptized by white sound turning colors at the
living edge, on the fringe of disenchantment. I like the realism
of Tom Petty and his Heartbreak sound of L.A. fantastic, and
the lost enchantment of Al Stewart's Nostradamus, the clear
epics drifting inside the head of a rock, like moss on a rolling
stone, there is the woman just like Tom Thumb, circling in the
air with diamonds. The minstrels sing of injustice, of the Fall
of America in the warped Masters of War, transposed upon
electric fever. Or the electric cool-aid acid tests transplanted in
Jimi Hendrix's imagination, warped by a purple haze. Or the
fresh taste of Cream, and its marshmallow side-kick, with a
prayer for God to buy her a mercedes benz, with reds pawned
for a midnight with the Queen of funk. The lucid learings of
Pink Floyd encapsulated by the Wall, wearing funeral ties for
the British Empire. The royal son in drag, like a gypsie with
big fat lips rolling down a hill with well rounded Stones. The
Church of the Electric Guitar in a frenzy doing a wedding for
the middleman of brave sorcery, discussing anarchy in the
back room behind the pews. What is commercial rock, but the
blind and arrogant hypocrisy of an inheritance to the Rolling
Thunder, with undeserved applause. Here the shattered dreams
of synthetic disco, and the binding of jazz at the peanut gallery.
The cynics of blind justice rage in turn, while the melting pot
gets hotter. The Moody Blues with its smooth announcement of
the early death of LSD's punk hero. The Godadavita with fleas
raging on its electric neck, singing with pressed lips to a window
of disenfranchisement. The political ills are the pressure cooker
heating up into an electric jam. Like Peter Gabriel and Biko,
let the murdered seek their voice in the living. Iron Butterfly
in siege with flames, lurking for the lost buffalo of an extinct

dream. And the Grateful Dead are leaning on the pot smoke horizon, looking down on a sea of green fish.

UNIVERSAL PLEASURE

Urn for thinkers
Utopia of false dreams
Unburdened children
Understudy of affluence
Unquestionable delights
Unconscious as machines
Unanimously fed
Ungrateful matriculates
Urizen gone
Unearthed souls that monster reason
Uniform in thought
Unauthentic poets
Unauthorized dreamers
Unexperienced Christians denouncing the Cross
Unborn betrayers of vision
Unenthralled learners
Unction of their words flowing
Urinated for a Professor's eye
Unclaimed baggage of the Heart
Ultra-ignorance dressed in the garb of knowledge
Unbuddha
Ulcers of love
Unrealized Soul lost in labyrinths
Unwed Soul and angelic mourner before the death of God
Undenounced denouncers
Unthought nihilism
Undetermined maya like a coronet for education
Unopinionated politicians
Unfucked whores of knowledge
Unreduced teachers with see thru dresses
Unzipped passions
Uncle Sam's Playground
Ungodly gluttons like Caligula feasting upon his horses head
Uncorrupted Fausts
Unchaste virgins
Undying with Mcphisto's pen in hand
Unblind Sauls struck down
Unrecognition of the True One

Union of Serpentary science participating in the murder of Buddha
Unworshiped primadonnas of dictionaries
Upheaval of pariahs
Upon His Cross the dogs beg for Vision
USA summer camp of love to teach the blind ones the price of their
    eyes now sold
to darkness.

UNTITLED

from that tiny cup
into the tank little
sips of water
no matter they are still
dying their tails bent
like spoons are messages
of that cold death
their backs are burnt
and charred bone
then in the schoolyard
I realize they are too
small to live
they know only the
solitude of angels
the still moon childlike
in its constant loving
of the Sun from
its shroud of balloons
you are hiding
always intelligent
with young playmates
you rest in the dark
conifer of birth
dark sleep of wood
for other animals of
light.

VISIT

Talking with my mom,
she drove all the way up to Eureka
from Aptos California.
We spent the day together chatting,
conversing, reading poems, acknowledging
that the season is the depth of an early autumn
painted with fog and mist,
deep as the bird that flies through smokestacks
penetrating the sky with its wings.
I smoke a cigarette and my mother pours coffee
from her traveling companion coffee-maker
We adjust, tease and laugh at pictures of me at
six with tomahawk raised in a New Mexico church
that we stayed in one deep Easter.
We talk of my nephew, how he is just growing
and growing, we talk of the home she has just
purchased in New Mexico. We drive to Old Town,
wandering in used clothes stores.
At St. Vincent De Paul's I try on shirts for
my brother who is going to the Philippines to
find a wife. Strictly cotton so he can sweat and
remain cool. We laugh about him, wondering if his
bride will love him, or does she just want to come
to America?
I dance inside, fresh new dreams,
I tell her of Rimbaud, of my new poems,
And she buys me a birthday present, Dylan's Infidels.
We go out to Japanese food after hanging out in her room
drinking crystal Geysers with cherry flavored water,
and smoking cigs. Till we both cough.
She older now, but poised between the civil and the fancy,
a kind of tactful lady who is well preserved, and very healthy.
We eat our dinner talking of Death, the Void, the absence
of things we cannot imagine. She does not believe in God,
but lives an ethical life. I visit, talk of women I have
loved, and feel my belly, it is full of tempura.
We eat till we are stuffed. I imagine her trip back,
A long drive. I give her a kiss as she drops me off,

back home I feel the wind in my heart, the wind dancing, moving with absolution, and I find words again to speak of the chemical dust that is light in my forehead. Home and happy that our visit went well.

WESTERN STAR

From the Black pit
of Industry; the snail
of common growth
with its shell of solid light
goes climbing the mountains
of America, finding solitude
on the nameless beaches
of California,
I have come to a Western world,
I have meditated on the eternal flower
of Selfdom, and like the snail of poverty
I have found aloneness in action.
Turning ocean, your tide is birth
drowning out the shouts of death,
the old man is changing, soon dusk
will fall upon the water.
I have looked at America, and seen the steel
salute of ignorant machinery cut night down
to pieces.
This Earth is raining suicide,
yet it is alive with rare exquisite beauty
made into a form by Man that is nakedness
without tranquility. To buy the death-maker's
dreams, is to sell out the future.
I have traveled West to see the shinning star of
Industry snuffed like a candle in the middle of
its struggle to be free.

WHAT FOLLOWS US

Peace flows through the streets,
the light is like a glove around the parking meters,
time is measured in distances,
we burn into the darkness like candles
that suffocate in the dawn of light
we are fixtures, forever portraying ourselves,
spent like magnets in the birth of memory,
I fail to write the poem that is writing me,
I ride the wind upon a sack of paper,
I see the sky and its rainbow pressed upon its back,
there are people everywhere, flirting children and bees
full of pollen, the flowers are needy,
we belong at second glance, we eat ice-cream cones
and cherish the first image that comes to our heads,
there are no icons that last,
only the flaunting of silence is stable,
cold flies in warm air,
these things that flow are one step behind the things
that are stationary, the real is only a love of illusion,
we are born perfecting the stars,
ice is merged with fire to form one body,
the way is centered in the smoke,
tomorrow I am closer to than yesterday,
the poem writes itself,
I follow.

WHAT NOBODY SAW

Not him, bold like a phantom,
or the blood running cold, the rude
awakening that silence is the essence of all
things, the slap in the face, the meaningless
trial where the court-machine rambled on,
two mirrors handcuffed together, dancing;
a bathroom semi-private cutting wrist, cigarettes
dollar bills, they said: "Everything is for sale,"
but nobody thought to take them literally, except
the wise-man and his bogus inter-change, then they called
to their masters: "Cut them Down!", they raped the Land,
they caused the soul to bleed, but nobody ever figured it
out, a crushed heart-beat upon a lit piece of paper,
a fragrant garden smashed in its iron mill, the sand screaming
in the eyes of blood and water, and they walked a little wobbly
like ancient dinosaurs, there were movies, many of them,
but the little monopoly board kept growing, so they borrowed
from the culture of their offspring, they centered themselves
in their chair of supreme command, and talked on their radio
phones, while the court ran up its budget, and the homeless
stood teary-eyed inside museums of the future, we tugged
at the rope, but nobody could hold it, we saw the encounter
with the vampire of spare-change, but nobody could use it,
then we sank below the flames, blaming everything on everybody
else, shouting to the night and its hidden camera that we
were framed, while silent pictures are taken of the shrunken
heads, smiling teeth bare as a rose garden with its thorny
eyes waking in the simple hands of morning.

WHAT TIME IS IT?

When will you see
that Time doesn't exist?
shifting polarities, eyes
without words, parting silences,
concave Worlds, laughter
at midnight, the white walls
reflect a mirror from which you
come strolling in asking what
Time is it?
We roll, we flow, we jitter,
we chat in cafes full of time.
Turn, the clock half-past whatever,
cooking dinner I realize that time
is necessary in planning a meal,
but I will wait, wait for everything to happen,
the smell of herb baked chicken,
the casual boiling of rice,
the bread in the oven, smelling of
warmth, I wait, and like the man bent
over a mirror I wonder what time it is.

WINTER SOLSTICE

The long shadow touches the earth
the Sun hides its face in the southern hemisphere,
the ice lies thick on car windows,
the wind is bitter cold,
it hugs my ears and my cheeks go blue,
tonight I watched a convoy of trucks
drive down Broadway with Christmas lights on
and Santa Claus waving back,
I drank warm coffee and talked with a friend,
the year is getting thin,
soon it will be nineteen ninety,
what have we accomplished,
I mean us: humanity where are we going,
the long shadow will gradually recede, and Spring
will chase its tail,
Summer will dance in daylight,
but now it is icy and cold,
no rain has come for weeks,
where are we going, I mean the whole human race,
one more decade old and what have we done???
Let us pass the earth unto our children, but
what kind of earth are we passing?
This generation has fucked things up;
the new generation must deal with the whole damn
mess we've left the world in.
The long shadow is melting down, the green house
is growing around the earth like an iron lung;
people are still starving everywhere, and it's winter
and the homeless have no where to go.
Back East they sleep in subways or build bonfires
for the coldest weather they've seen in years. I am
grateful for my life, I feel I have accomplished
things. Another decade and more promise.
The earth's shadow is dressed in black,
It has an appointment with the Sun.
The shortest day of the year has come.

WRITTEN TO JONI MITCHELL'S
COURT AND SPARK

The work
stroking star making machinery
beneath the popular song
the flesh of doves and the dreamers
caught in the City of Lost Angels
coming alive I remember my childhood hearing
these songs smoky rings in the sky
leaves like flying saucers bending
in the windy day fresh redwood cones
and the songs blasting from the stereo
as my mother clips her roses
the rum voice of solitary wind
streams through the speakers
I concentrate listen like a sharpened
needle going down the black grooves
listening to the come down and look at
the trains meeting in People's Park
strange shadow man in his missing car
everybody waiting
old man sleeping on his back
Jesus running in a silver tinted meadow
of warm dogs panting breath through jazz phones
what brings me back to the dark listening
with my father spread out in his favorite chair
by the fire
water whispering in the drain
clickety clack
drums and flutes in speakers of silence
like death but better
butter between bread
Court & Spark.

YOU AND I

I read on the bathroom walls
'the walls have ears'
so I am borrowing this from the red paint,
I have decided to tell no secrets
without first bowing to them,
bedding them down with sweet water
and wanting lullaby to brow beat sleep
that I do not know the ears of the sleeper
does not disturb me,
for all the laws of dreaming are borrowed
from a hollow place where you can hear
the body echo against itself,
eclipse and revivify the closed circle of meat,
for sometimes under blue moon days
the meat talks to itself, uttering cold ellipses
of triangular passions, occult circumstance,
it bends forward in an inventive sway
to mumble a name of some coldly abstract animal
cased in a ball of glass,
an exodus that remembers its strangers walk
leg by leg,
a final drawing of the footsteps
behind the hidden wall, with only the slightest
suggestion of burial,
mostly copying the neck of a phoenix
bidden down in flame...
A textile sandbox
tells us obsequiously how to
bend our knees,
making sense out of hieroglyphic company
with our red-bucket play of scabby kiss
and feeling up the dress
to boob a smile with raped teeth,
and when we decide who's who in the play,
after all I could be St. Catherine riding
her hollow horse to battle
or Charlie Brown turning his blockhead smile
windward to the dope of night,

riding a brand new tricycle
through the legs of her red hair,
talking about origins
as if they were names to be dropped,
delicious sounding, with full demi-god force,
and black hands that Erasmus ordered.
I come for you.

AFTERWORD BY NEELI CHERKOVSKI

Eric Walker jumped into my life so quickly and with so much 18-year-old wonder and abandon that I had trouble understanding where his poems came from, nor did I realize their enduring value. The poets of San Francisco took Eric for the wild and free-wheeling poet he would always be in his short life. Eric was a spark plug for the scene. He could turn a quiet cafe into a den of poetic thought and for that everyone was quietly thankful.

The first evening we met he spoke of the importance of William Everson in his life. Not only did he draw sustenance from Everson's *The Birth of a Poet*, but he had the opportunity of sitting in on the poet's classes at UC Santa Cruz, awed by this tall, bearded man whose spiritual journey and poetic growth came about on the same terrain Eric knew so well. Everson's plain-spoken instructions dwelt on an Emerson-inspired self-reliance, and on his aggressive connection with man on the land. Eric and I read aloud both the thunderous poems of Everson's life as Brother Antoninus and from the later work with its return to the more nature-oriented imagery of his youth.

In the days of late 1982 and early '83, Eric's was a wily and slim, somewhat gawky presence. How I remember them, those eyes, the eyes of a poet for sure, restless, probing, bespeaking an intelligence, viewing the world through poetic lashes. Poetry wasn't just art for Eric Walker, it was his bread and wine. He would come to ravage my Harwood Alley bookshelf, finding gems inside of gems, gold inside of gold. Among them were *Nightwood* by Djuna Barnes, *Ace of Pentacles* by John Wieners, and an early Charles Bukowski poetry collection inscribed to me. I saw that this high school dropout knew where to find a true classroom: in his own hands, out of his own mind. I read a few poems to Eric hoping to elicit an enthusiastic response. "You use the word 'time' too much. I'd watch that." "What do you mean?" I asked. "Well, think of a melting clock, like in the Dalí painting. You can describe time and not have to use the word so much."

As we talked over the months to come, I observed that for all his antics, and there were many—the time he doused me with a water balloon while I sat in our favorite cafe, the day he stole a bag of books from our local bookstore—I also remember him listening acutely to what was going on around him and taking notes when someone said something interesting. This was a poet who caught the rhythms of ordinary speech, who identified them within the lyrical chamber of his own mind, and was able to construct poems with a relentless passion largely out of what he conjured. I knew then that his personal taste would carry him down surrealism's path, grabbing the outrageous image, smoothing it down to a fine lyrical glow. He had an intense feeling for the commonplace as well. Eric was simply 'out there' on a breeze-driven night in the poetic whole.

The phone rang one day and it was Philip Lamantia who had heard a young poet had landed in town. In no time Philip came over and was sitting at the kitchen table. Eric was in heaven, facing a man whose earliest poetic efforts at fourteen had been recognized by the likes of André Breton. They shared a natural enthusiasm. Philip the elder was still Philip the younger—restless and feverish. Anyone listening that morning would have seen an elder youth with the wisdom of the ages and from whom the young poet could learn. He spoke with grim authority of the French Surrealists, often pounding the table to make a point. Eric had met his match and he knew it—offering Philip his last cigarette. What Philip went on to delineate, as he expounded, was a map to such Surrealist precursors as Matthew Lewis, Gérard de Nerval, and Lautréamont. He also added a few words of praise for the English poet Thomas Chatterton who had taken his own life while still in his teens. At this point, Eric might easily have fallen off his chair so intoxicated was he, as Lamantia grew increasingly excited. I went over and ground enough coffee for a strong pot as Philip launched into a new frenetic discourse, on alchemy.

Over the ensuing months Eric came to know North Beach culture well. We raced one another to the Caffe Trieste, eager for our coffee, eager for our friends, and just plain eager. "Come on, old man, come on" he would encourage as we made our way past the venerable Italian businesses sagging in the San Francisco light. Eric became the darling of Yolanda, the sister of the cafe's founder, Gianni Giotto. Often she would dote on him as he hopped, skipped, and jumped table to table as Puccini or Verdi boomed out of the juke box. In no time Eric was rubbing shoulders with Kirby Doyle, Bob Kaufman, and Gregory Corso—heady heroes for a kid from Santa Cruz who was sewing his way into the fabric of poetry. You felt his exuberance, and admired the commitment to his journey—at one minute in animated conversation with the political lyricist Jack Hirschman and with the translator George Scrivani, or charming a young French woman from Paris, then eagerly listening to her description of the Left Bank. Caffe Trieste was a mixture of downtown business people, successful cultural figures, secret poets, world travelers, and a stopping-place for Allen Ginsberg on his jaunts through town. For Lawrence Ferlinghetti it served as an anteroom to his office at City Lights Publishing Company. When Eric met him, introduced by me one morning, Ferlinghetti smiled kindly and said, "Welcome to the Casbah."

When witnessing Eric's often over-the-top behavior, it was not difficult to wonder about his mental stability. By the waning days of our time together I realized he needed help, but said nothing as he was not about to listen. His clothing became more and more flamboyant, his talk was often scattered, words shooting out staccato-like over the table, and he exhibited some truly paranoid traits: he was being stopped from publication; people were conspiring against him; he was going to leave and never come back. Still, the writing kept on coming—a growing body of illuminating work.

It astounds me now, decades later, that Eric was gone by age twenty-nine. I do not remember the circumstances of our parting, other than that it was devastating for me but that it was also a way to free myself of another poet's aura. I needed my own space, and because Eric was bouncing off the walls with his rapidly developing psychological problems, I groped for silence. For some reason, when he would call from distant places, even from Eureka, where he took his own life, badgered by the police and plagued with delusions, a toxic combination, I either didn't take his calls or spoke quickly and abruptly. Only when his magnificent poems surfaced through the work of Tisa Walden, who had published him initially, and Raymond Foye via his tribute in the *Brooklyn Rail*, did I come to appreciate him anew. Walden came to know Eric early on, and from the beginning, appreciated his gift. She would publish four of Walker's books, *Night's Garden*, *Helen*, *Jonah's Song*, and *Notes of a Surrealist*. They were beautifully produced chapbooks over-brimming with lyrical energy. Another book was in the planning stages, but fell through.

I feel fortunate to have had so many poets in my life: Charles Bukowski when I was fifteen and beyond, and then with Eric in my late 30s. I hold a candle out to both of them: two ends, many ends, amends and amen. The poems of Eric Walker are exquisite. Not only did he possess a musical ear and a natural sense of craft, but he left behind a considerable body of work. Although repetitive at times, that in itself only enhances the sense of mastery in the written work when he prevails over his inner demons. It also gives the reader a presentment of what might have risen to the surface later, if his life had not been so tragically shortened. They are so much of his mind and of his imagination, but they grew out of the rough and beautiful coast lands of California, and down through the tangled shadows of his psychic redwood forest. He is a poet of revelation.